Collywobbles: Tales of Travel, Life, and Anxiety

FAYE BRENNER

Collywobbles: Tales of Travel, Life, and Anxiety
Faye Brenner

Published by
Hybrid Global Publishing
301 E. 57th Street, 4th Floor
New York, New York 10022

Author: Brenner, Faye
Title of Book: Collywobbles: Tales of Travel, Life, and Anxiety
ISBN: 978-1-951943-48-6
eBook: 978-1-951943-49-3

Cover Design by Jonathan Pleska
Author Photo by Chris Richman

www.fayebrenner.com

CONTENTS

PREFACE

'I know how to take care o' myself: not the first time I've had a run of the squitters and collywobbles. Amitav Ghosh, *Sea of Poppies*

Collywobbles. *Shpilkes.* It doesn't matter what I call it. I have always been anxious.

Sometime in the beginning of the 21st century, I sat in my doctor's examination room complaining about an ailment, now forgotten, when he changed the conversation.

"Are you nervous?"

"No, why?"

"Because you're making me nervous."

It wasn't the first time we had this conversation. Dr. Ryan was convinced that I suffered from anxiety, but I wasn't ready to accept his diagnosis.

It's not as though there hadn't been indications as long as I can remember. I was often absent from school because of bellyaches that, with hindsight, were a manifestation of my anxiety or the *collywobbles*, a British term that comes from "colic" and "wobbles." I like the sound of the word. It softens the reverberation of generalized anxiety disorder.

In high school I thought about backing out of my first international trip because of severe abdominal pain that turned out to be nothing more than angst. It was *shpilkes*, which translates to the feeling of "sitting on pins and needles" in Yiddish, the amazingly expressive language of my ancestors. It embodies the feeling I get in my head when I am a bundle of nerves. Stress releases hormones that send blood up to my brain, causing a tingling sensation in different parts of my body, but mostly around my skull. I was sure that I was dying. I have always been a hypochondriac.

The sensation of "pins and needles" wasn't the only physical manifestation of my *shpilkes*. Before flying, I also suffered the wrath of Montezuma's Revenge, squitters like the skipper of the *Ibis* in *Sea of Poppies*. There is a scientific reason anxiety causes diarrhea. My body is preparing me for survival by getting rid of all the junk in my digestive system so that it can send much needed blood to my brain to keep me from getting too wobbly, and it will take it from any place it can.

Despite belly aches and other manifestations of anxiety, I travel. A misguided marriage impelled my desire for globetrotting, and my resourcefulness overcame my lack of funds. Through four careers – as a teacher, a residential summer camp director, an educational administrator, and, finally, as a tour director – I have been privileged to journey throughout the world. My addiction to travel supersedes any anxiety, yet, my *shpilkes* also defines my globetrotting experience. These are the tales of my travels with the collywobbles.

1

FLYING FOIBLES

The difficulty lay with the mind accommodating itself to the notion of the plane, with all its weight, defying gravity, staying aloft. She understood the aerodynamics of flight, could comprehend the laws of physics that made flight possible, but her heart, at the moment, would have none of it. Her heart knew the plane could fall out of the sky.

Anita Shreve, *The Pilot's Wife*

When I picked up a copy of Erica Jong's *Fear of Flying* at my college book store I was more curious to read about the "zipless fuck" – anonymous, satisfying sex with a stranger – than the narrator's flying phobia. Chatter about the "zipless fuck" was rampant on my college campus on Long Island in 1973. I had recently lost my virginity, and the thought of having sex with a handsome nameless gentleman in an elevator aroused my newly discovered sexual awareness.

As the novel opens, Isadora Wing is flying to Vienna from New York with 117 psychoanalysts, including her husband. Despite thirteen years of therapy, Isadora is still afraid of flying. As the plane takes off, her fingers turn to ice, her stomach feels as though it is moving up to her throat, and her nipples harden. Her husband unsuccessfully attempts to calm her fear by holding her cold hand. As the plane passes over Jamaica Bay on its ascent, Isadora Wing is in a state of panic. When the "No Smoking" sign goes off, the narrator is still afraid that the plane is going to burst into "flaming pieces." At the time, I was more interested in the heroine's sexual exploits than her fear of flying. I wanted to be like Isadora Wing, who wasn't merely flying, but stretching her wings.

Three years after discovering the literary "zipless fuck," I was married to my college boyfriend, Paul. There had been no anonymous sex along the way, and, unfortunately, I found myself in a marriage dominated by my husband's need for control.

One weekend afternoon I announced that I was going to the mall. I didn't really need anything except a temporary escape.

"Paul, I'm going to the mall."

"What for?"

"Nothing, I just want to get out for a while."

"If you don't need anything, there is no reason to go the mall. You'll just end up spending money."

"I'm going."

I wasn't as brave as Isadora, but I was determined. He tried to stop me again.

"I really don't care what you think," and with that I walked out of our second-floor garden apartment and down the stairs to our only car.

He followed. "I said there is no reason to go to the mall."

"You are not my father," and with that, I closed the car door and turned the key.

As Paul reached for the door handle, I drove away, catching the disbelief on his face as he led a brief chase on foot. My shopping excursion was a fleeting break, but I would soon find a better escape through travel.

Paul was frustrated by what he perceived was my lack of appreciation for money. He saved. I spent. It costs money to travel, and he insisted that our budget didn't leave any funds for such frivolity. I was determined to find a way to travel despite him. When I discovered I was able to indulge my wanderlust with free international trips simply by signing up a group of students for an educational tour, Paul lost his argument to hold me back.

Less than a year later, I was flying over Jamaica Bay with a group of students on our way to London on a whirlwind European tour as one of two teacher chaperones. The other was my colleague, Carolyn, who would become my dear friend and travel companion. I was anxious about flying, although not panic-stricken like Isadora on her way to Vienna. Butterflies fluttered in my gut, but after the pilot turned off the "No

Smoking" and seat belt signs, I relaxed. I downed a couple of glasses of cheap red wine and fell asleep to the sounds of students chattering in anticipation.

Two hours later a raspy announcement woke me from an alcohol-induced slumber.

"Ladies and gentlemen, this is your Captain speaking. I regret to inform you that we have lost one of our engines."

I wasn't sure if I heard him correctly, so I turned to Carolyn and asked, "What did he say?"

She held her pointer finger up to her mouth as if to say, "Shut up and listen to what the man is saying. We might die."

"I want to assure you that this 747 is designed to fly without one of its four engines. However, in order to maintain the highest level of safety, we will be returning to New York."

We were almost halfway to Heathrow.

"We will be making a small descent before diverting the plane to JFK. Rest assured that we have everything under control."

"If we were halfway to London, why not simply continue in that direction?" I asked of no one in particular, but Carolyn was in ear-shot, so she answered.

"I don't know, but I am sure there is a good reason. I think we need to remain calm. If we panic, the kids will panic."

Carolyn was a master of composure, but I was going into full-panic mode. The familiar feeling of my stomach pushing itself up into my rib cage was met with an unfamiliar feeling of my fingers and toes turning to ice. Yet, I didn't want to be a nuisance by pushing the call button when everyone was just as clueless. The flight attendants had better things to do than assuage my anxiety, but I eventually caught the attention of a stewardess as she walked past my seat. This was before we had flight attendants.

"Why are we going back to New York? Why don't we just go to Heathrow? If we can fly safely, then why are we returning?" I don't know how to ask one question at a time, especially flying in a plane that is about to drop out of the sky.

She explained with a composed voice, "The loss of one engine makes it a bit more difficult to maintain altitude, so the ride might be a little bumpy. The final descent will be quick, and we will be landing without the reversal power of all four engines. We are returning to JFK because they are better equipped to handle emergency landings."

I didn't like her answer.

Isadora Wing resorts to alcohol to ease her fear of flying. I feel an affinity for a woman who rationalizes that, drunk, "You still believe you're going to die whenever the sound of the engines changes, but you don't care anymore." I drank another glass of wine. I made the absurd decision to get drunk on a plane that was in danger of crashing.

Taking a cue from Carolyn, I tried to hide my fear from our teenage charges, including my sister Reneé, a high school senior at the time.

My sister asked me if I was okay.

"Sure, why?"

"You look terrified." Perhaps she mistook "tanked-up" for terrified.

I kept repeating to myself, "Please let the plane land safely. Please let the plane land safely." I wasn't praying to God. I was attempting to control the pilots and the plane through positive thinking. I took my cue from Isadora who kept concentrating very hard, "helping the pilot…fly the 250-passenger mother-fucker." I had to concentrate almost twice as hard since this motherfucker was carrying 416 passengers.

Just in case of the unthinkable, I decided to say my goodbyes to my family. I fished through my carry-on to find my red-covered journal that still sits on a shelf in my office. I thought these might be my last words to my loved ones, hoping that the lined pages expressing my love might survive even if I didn't. After scribbling details about the situation, I ended the account of our calamity with a declaration of love for Paul. "I love him and want him. I really am still very scared and frightened of not making it at all." I was referring to my plunging to death, not the eventual descent of our marriage. They say that absence makes the heart grow fonder, but so does the fear of death.

I continued to drink. Having my senses intact would have been the more sensible thing to do considering that I was accompanying impressionable young people on our journey. Being sober in a crash landing might also be a good idea. At least the wine let me sleep for a couple of hours. By the time we were ready to land, I was in alert mode.

Our landing instructions were anything but routine.

"Ladies and gentlemen, as we make our final descent, we ask you to take the brace position: heads down and hands over your head. You are advised to remove your glasses before bracing."

A glimpse of the fire engines, ambulances, and police cars lining the runway belied the calm voice of the flight attendant. The captain didn't land. Instead, he pulled back up and circled the airport before making a second approach. As soon as we hit the runway, we felt the reverse thrusters doing everything in their power to stop the plane. The jolting of the aircraft made it difficult to maintain the crash position. When we finally came to a standstill on the tarmac, there was no bodily harm, just frayed nerves.

Once we were inside the terminal, my brain went from fright to action mode. It was after midnight, and I had to get ten students, Carolyn, and me to London. Determined to book our group on the first available flight, I pushed my way to the front of the line of weary travelers waiting for new flights. A majority of the passengers were proceeding to Bombay, requiring double rebooking. While Carolyn remained calm, I became illogically assertive.

"I have ten young people...we need to get to London," I said, as though we were more important than all of the others waiting for a way out of New York. Carolyn gently reminded me that everyone else was as anxious to get to their destinations as we were.

We were eventually booked on an early morning departure to London on the now defunct TWA. Although Air India offered us a hotel, Carolyn and I agreed that we could all catch a little more shut eye at the airport than if we dragged ten teenagers to a cheap motel in Queens. We grabbed our bags and transferred by bus to Eero Saarinen's revolutionary TWA terminal where we transformed the red vinyl benches into beds and their cushions into pillows and settled in for a restless night before taking to the skies again.

As we waited at the departure gate for our early morning flight, I conceived a travel ritual that remains a part of my international travel protocol. I aimed my point-and-shoot camera at the plane and clicked. My convoluted reasoning was that collecting photographs of the airplanes that flew me around the world made it far less likely that one of them might drop out of the sky.

Travel rituals are not unusual. Some people begin each trip with a shot of tequila before boarding. Others offer a prayer for safe travels. My daughter always buys a copy of *The Economist* for light reading on the flight. She fears the dire consequences if she fails to pick up a copy. I have never asked her what she would do if she had two international flights in one month. Nobody needs two copies of *The Economist*. At the very least, my pictures of airplanes make a great first photo in my travel albums.

Rituals, however, can also produce anxiety. For example, like any smart traveler, I check to be sure I have my passport securely in my bag before leaving the house. Next, I verify its presence on each leg of the journey: the car, taxi, or the shuttle bus from the long-term parking lot. Upon arrival at the airport, I verify its location one more time before checking in. It is common sense that, if a passport is in your bag when you leave the house, it will still be there in the Uber and, again, when you arrive at the airport. Anxiety, however, has nothing to do with common sense.

Over forty years after our plane almost crashed, I took an Uber to the Raleigh-Durham Airport the first time I flew overseas after retiring to North Carolina. I followed my routine, checking my passport before leaving the house, and once again on the way to the airport in the car. Yet, on the third check, it was gone. After emptying my handbag on the terminal floor, I panicked. My hands started to sweat, and my heart rate was out of control. The only logical explanation was that I dropped it in the car.

I texted my driver, and, when I didn't receive a reply, I texted Uber. There was a long silence, producing a knot in my chest. Finally, my cell phone dinged with a message that Uber was still trying to contact the driver. Although I was steadfast in my belief that I had put the passport back into my purse, I looked inside my carry-on bag. Through the steady trickle of tears, I spotted the imitation snakeskin passport holder. Just as I pulled it out, another ding on my phone informed me that the driver had searched his car and that, of course, the passport wasn't there. It was in my hand. Rather than putting it back into my purse in the Uber, I had carelessly tossed it into my carry-on. You would think someone with anxiety about losing a passport would take better care of it. I didn't catch my breath until we boarded the plane.

I discovered a traditional Jewish ritual on my first trip to Israel when one of my friends offered me a dollar and told me to give it to a needy person once we landed. She said it was *Shaliach Mitzvah*. It's also called "passing the buck." According to Jewish tradition, a traveler has extra protection if she is on a journey to perform a *mitzvah*, or good deed. By donating the dollar, I would be safeguarded on my trip. With my photo of the El Al plane snapped and my dollar in hand, I was ready to fly.

It was 1993, and I was traveling with a group of Jewish religious school teachers on an educational tour of Israel to study its history, culture, and people, with the goal of improving the Israeli curriculum of our schools, or, in my case, of the residential summer camp that had just hired me as their director. Before we departed, our group leader, Rabbi Jacob Halpern, led us in the traveler's prayer, *Tefilat Haderach*. Standing in a circle at the gate, we beseeched God to rescue us from any enemy, ambush, or any punishment that may come upon us in our travels. We asked to reach our destination filled with life, peace, and gladness. I think we covered all the bases. I may not be a believer, but such invocations can't hurt. Now, nothing was going to prevent us from a safe journey.

Our overnight flight from JFK to Tel Aviv's Ben Gurion Airport was primarily uneventful. After I managed a couple of hours' sleep, the sun began to peek through the window shade. I was only half awake when I noticed that most of the men were standing and turning toward the back of the plane. The orthodox men blessed and kissed their *tallit*, or prayer shawls, before tossing them around their shoulders. They donned their *tefillin*, a religious article that looks like a little black hat with leather straps on each side.

The "hat" is actually a small box that contain four written texts from the Bible which, when praying, are bound "as a sign upon your hand and they shall be for a reminder between your eyes." The men placed one black strap on their left arm, wrapping it in a precise manner around their arm, hand, and fingers and the other on their forehead. They turned to the East and davened their morning prayer.

I had never witnessed this type of devotion. I envied the strength of their spiritual belief while still feeling a sense of the absurdity of these men wearing black leather straps wrapped around their arms with the tiny box on their foreheads. These were my people, but their rituals were foreign to me. I didn't really believe that a photo protected a plane from crashing or that a prayer kept us safe, but these men had true faith. My practices were superstition, not religious conviction.

However, the rituals worked. As the wheels of the plane touched the ground, most everyone erupted in cheers and joyous clapping. They do that on El Al. People have an emotional attachment to the land of Israel. I saw travelers kneel down and kiss the ground as they reached the end of the airstair. I felt the palpable excitement of arriving in Israel, until I arrived at immigration and customs.

Israel relies on the human factor to keep its passengers safe: the scrutiny of the security guards. These young men and women, most of whom have just completed their mandatory military service, concentrate on the individual traveler rather than the water they forgot in their bag or the shoes they happen to be wearing. When the gentleman with the Uzi engaged me in a penetrating conversation, my anxiety escalated more than any time I had to take off my shoes or turn over my too-large bottle of face cream after 9/11.

Usually when I arrive in a country the customs officer might ask me how long I plan to stay, where I am visiting, and whether my visit is for pleasure or business. I wasn't prepared for Israeli customs.

"Do you speak Hebrew?" asked the soldier sporting an Uzi around his chest.

"Just a few words." If I was supposed to remain calm, he was making it very difficult.

"Why not? Didn't you go to Hebrew School?"

I didn't think that was any of his business, but I gave him a truthful answer, "No."

"Why didn't your parents send you to Hebrew School?"

Now I was speechless. Was I supposed to tell him that we were a lower middle-class family without the means to join a synagogue? Or should I say that my parents didn't think it was necessary for a young girl to have a Bat Mitzvah and saw no purpose in sending me three times a week to religious school? Or that my mother didn't drive, was often sick, and car-pooling was too difficult? Or that I actually resented the fact that I didn't go to religious school with my friends? None of those answers sufficed, so I said, "I don't know."

I passed the interrogation, and the officer allowed me to enter into his country. When I met my fellow travelers on the other side, they explained to me that he didn't care about the answers. The security guard was engaging me in conversation, observing how I reacted. This first trip to Israel generated a new anxiety about flying – immigration. My pulse doesn't slow until I am safely heading out of the international airport.

Four years later, on a camp staffing trip to Israel, I arrived at the Ben Gurion Airport ready for my interrogation, only to find myself sans suitcase. I fought off the collywobbles with a trick I had learned early in my teaching career at a professional development seminar on handling stress. The workshop leader shared a technique to control our reactions to problems we face.

He set up a scenario: "You have just arrived on vacation, and the airline has lost your bag." Hindsight makes that quite an apropos example. "You are angry at the airlines, and you think your vacation is ruined. You wonder how you are going to enjoy yourself without all of the items and clothes you packed for your holiday. Now, I want you to think of a scale of 1 to 10. Let's make the Holocaust a 10. Now where is your problem on this scale?"

I put my lost bag on the scale and decided it was a one. Today I would probably put it as a zero, but that's what happens when you become an old hand at losing luggage.

It was Friday morning, and I had the weekend to relax in Tel Aviv before starting to interview potential staff Monday morning. Most of the markets would be closing early for Shabbat, so, after checking into my hotel, I headed straight to the Carmel Market, the largest collection of produce and clothing vendors in the city. The *Shuk Hacarmel*, as it is known in Hebrew, dates back to 1920, before Israel became a country.

I didn't have much time to shop before it closed, but I picked up basic items to clothe me through the next few days: a pair of clogs, which were popular in the 90s, a dress to wear for the interviews, brown overalls with a beige shirt to wear underneath, and the staples—pajamas, socks, and underwear. In addition to clogs, overalls became a fad of the decade, a comfortable and casual outfit, perfect for travel, although I now think I look pretty silly in the photos. Overalls should only be worn by children and farmers.

I never did get my bag back while I was in Israel; it was delivered about six months later. It had fallen off the conveyor on its way to the plane at Dulles Airport, which was under construction at the time. It sat there the whole six months until, as the renovation was being completed, someone found it hiding under the old transporter. Not only did I receive compensation for the items in the suitcase, but I also received a check to cover everything I needed to purchase in Israel.

At least my luggage didn't take six months to find me in Scotland. I left Washington, D.C. for Scotland on a warm September afternoon in 2008. I was wearing short sleeves and sandals and had packed my sweaters, jacket, and umbrella. As we were nearing the Glasgow airport, an avuncular Scottish gentleman sitting to my right initiated a conversation with me.

"You are not exactly dressed for a day in Glasgow," he said. "Most of our days are filled with a cold mist or steady rain. There is a Scottish saying that there is no such thing as bad weather, only wrong clothes." I guess I was wearing the wrong clothes.

I thanked him for his insight, assuring him that I had the right clothes in my bag. Unfortunately, that suitcase never made it to the baggage claim. Once again, I assured myself that the situation was still at the very low end of the stress scale. After filling in the requisite forms to locate my luggage, I hailed a taxi to the Thistle Hotel in the city center, grateful that the Glasgow Airport delivers delayed baggage.

I shared my plight with the front desk, and the clerk assured me that they would let me know as soon as my bag arrived. He suggested I could pick up a few things just a few doors down at TK Maxx. At first I thought I didn't understand his brogue, but as I approached the store I saw the same iconic letters as our TJ Maxx at home. Not wanting to confuse the American store with the already established Scottish T.J. Hughes, the international company simply replaced the "J" with a "K." Everything else was the same, except for the prices in pound sterling. I bought a pair of boots, two sweaters, and pajamas.

My suitcase had yet to arrive by the morning. I found solace in the full Scottish breakfast of fried eggs, diagonally cut toast that was presented in a rack that resembled a taco holder, a banger, baked beans, and fresh fruit. By the time I finished breakfast, my bag was waiting for me at the front desk. Any need for an additional shopping spree was averted, and my Scottish gentleman friend would be glad to see me wearing the right clothes.

Three years later, I booked a mother-daughter trip to Morocco to celebrate the arrival of 2011 in this intriguing country in north Africa. My knowledge of Morocco, however, was limited to the classic movie, *Casablanca*, and cozy dinners at a local Moroccan restaurant, complete with floor seating and belly dancers, but without Sam on the piano playing "As Time Goes By." The local waiter brought rose-scented water to our table for us to wash our hands before using them to delve into our pastilla, a scrumptious appetizer with chicken layered into thin pastry sheets, similar to phyllo. The pie is a startling balance of sweet and savory with a layer of almonds, cinnamon, and sugar. I slowly devoured the pastilla, small bites at a time. When the tagine arrived, my stomach was full, but that has never stopped me from eating. Food tells the story of a place, and any country that had food this good was one I wanted to explore.

Since our flight to Morocco was departing from New York, I drove north from Virginia to spend a couple of days on Long Island with my father before we left. When we woke the next morning, New York was blanketed with thirty inches of snow in a rare December blizzard. By the first night of the storm, over 1,400 flights had been cancelled at the three New York airports, including the one in New Jersey. It's interesting that one of the New York airports is actually in a different state, but if the New York Giants can play in Jersey, I guess it's kosher.

The row of parked cars buried in white outside my dad's place revealed that we were not going anywhere any time soon. By the next day, the day of our departure, all of the airports on the Eastern seaboard were closed. Yet, I remained resolute, determined to get to Casablanca. I spent a portion of the day on hold with the tour operator as well as the airlines, with Christmas music playing in the background. I am a Jew who likes Christmas music. After all, some of the greatest Christmas songs were written by Jews: "A White Christmas," by Irving Berlin and Johnny

Marks' "Rudolph, the Red-Nosed Reindeer." However, someone forgot to tell the airlines that Christmas was over four days ago.

My father, ever the worrier, was apprehensive of us flying in the aftermath of the storm.

"I don't think you are going anywhere."

"Daddy, let's wait and see."

"I don't care if they open the airport or not. I don't want you to take a chance in this weather. Anyway, how are you going to get to the airport?" I was 56-years old, and my father still fretted about my safety. I didn't want to belittle his fears, so I bent the truth: "We won't go anywhere until we know we can get there safely."

The three of us waited eagerly for an update on our flight, one of us hoping that the airport never opened. Rachel, who was home in Brooklyn, was the stoic. She would love to get out of New York, but if we had to postpone the venture, we'd find another time to go. I continued to be unyielding: I was determined to get to Morocco. Rachel suggested I "chill out."

By the end of the day, our tour operator informed us that the only available flight was a pre-sunrise departure to Rome the next day with an overnight layover at a Leonardo da Vinci Airport hotel. With an option to pull out of the trip since we missed two days of the tour, Rachel and I decided to undertake the abbreviated adventure despite my father's misgivings. Mom and daughter bunked in a cheap airport hotel for the night and, with the requisite photo of our Alitalia plane, we took off on the journey to Morocco.

Since the tour included airfare from JFK, all eleven of us who braved the weather were delayed and rerouted through Rome, where we left our suitcases in the hands of Alitalia, grabbed our carry-ons, and bedded down in the airport hotel for the evening. Two days after schedule, we finally arrived in Casablanca. All eleven pieces of luggage, however, were M.I.A.

Since none of us spoke Arabic or Berber, they allowed our tour director, Hassan, to join us inside baggage claim. The airport staff offered little assistance other than taking down the tag numbers of the suitcases and Hassan's mobile phone number. The airport in Casablanca had not yet entered the modern age of bag tagging and couldn't tell us if our luggage had arrived earlier or not at all. Instead, they ushered us to the lost baggage room where we rummaged around for our bags.

As I entered the chamber, I took a whiff, hastily squeezing my nostrils together in an attempt to block the dreadful stench of musty bags and animal waste. Assorted pieces of luggage were sharing the room with feral cats and flailing birds and one misplaced cockatoo. The salmon-crested bird was tied to the top of a bamboo cage. Although the cats were ignoring the bird, I was anxious that the unfortunate creature was not being fed. We had no idea how long the cockatoo had been perched on the birdcage, but since it was still there when we departed for home, I assume someone was nurturing our feathered friend.

After a thorough search of the land of lost luggage, none of us located our bags. There wasn't much else to do but grab our carry-ons that held everything we needed for the one night in Rome and follow Hassan out of the airport. We checked into the Hotel Golden Tulip Farah, not far from the port in the Derb Omar district of Casablanca. It didn't faze me that we were in a dodgy commercial area and without most of our belongings. I was in Morocco and it was New Year's Eve.

When we woke up the next morning for our departure to Fes, a city made famous by the eponymous cap, we were still sans suitcases. With no delivery of lost bags in Morocco, we returned to the malodourous chamber of lost luggage every two days, each time encountering the unfortunate cockatoo. And each time we found a few suitcases. First, there were three. A few days later four more pieces of luggage materialized, including mine. Two more lucky people discovered their bags before we took off on our flight home. The last two were gone with the wind, including Rachel's. We returned home, leaving the bird still clinging to its cage. It haunted my dreams for months.

Three months and a day after receiving a check from Alitalia Airlines for her lost luggage, Rachel's ravaged London Fog tweed suitcase arrived at her Brooklyn apartment. She said it was like Christmas in July when she opened the bag to discover her long-forgotten, newly purchased red boots and her favorite navy-blue pea coat. We couldn't imagine what animals had crushed it or what machines had ripped it apart. She did not return the check to the airline. After all, she should be compensated for her loss and suffering.

I don't need the airlines to give me the collywobbles: I am capable of triggering my own anxiety when flying. In the spring of 2019, I was traveling to Sicily with a disparate group of seven women – three of us leaving from Raleigh-Durham and the rest meeting us in Rome to catch our connecting flight to Palermo. As my friend Lisa, her sister Nancy, and I were waiting in the security line, we were joined by a canine security team weaving its way through the long line of passengers. I must have turned a frightening shade of white.

Lisa, one of the younger members of my senior community, looked at me with concern. "Is everything okay?"

I eyed the black Labrador who was closing in. Rationally, I knew that the sniffer dog was charged with keeping us safe from explosives, but my mind went back to the previous day, when, as I took my underwear out of my drawer, I noticed that it reeked from the sweet smell of the marijuana I had hid there. Without any time to do a load of laundry, I packed the skunky panties and forgot about them until I saw the dog. I assumed that Lisa and her sister were "cool," but I toned down my cursing so that the TSA canine handler couldn't hear me.

"My underwear smells like pot. What if the dog smells it?"

Lisa laughed before she started to wonder if she would acknowledge our friendship if I were apprehended. She planned on traveling to Sicily today, not on bailing me out of jail. But could one really go to jail for having underwear that smelled like pot? By now, Nancy was also in on my secret, and the three of us held our breath as the sniffer dog passively continued up the line. Just as I was beginning to relax, Nancy noticed that the canine team was making a second round. Once again, the dog was not interested in my underwear. Relieved that she didn't have to abandon me to TSA, Lisa snorted, and Nancy and I giggled. There is a thin line between anxiety and hilarity.

Ten days and a lot of pasta and cannolis later, we began our trip home to our various airports with a flight from Palermo to Rome. The three of us holding the secret of the skunky panties were flying to JFK before catching the final flight back to Raleigh-Durham. After settling in at the gate in New York, I closed my eyes to take a nap. I started singing to myself, as I often do to fall asleep.

A hundred bottles of beer on the wall,
a hundred bottles of beer.
Take one down and pass it around,
99 bottles of beer on the wall.

My brain was trying to imagine a wall of beer with a library ladder on which a faceless person was grabbing bottles and handing them to people – not to me because I don't drink beer. In the background I heard chatter about the weather in upstate New York. Someone mentioned our plane, which was coming in from Buffalo, was delayed by a storm. I never made it to the eighty-third bottle of beer. Instead, I concentrated on the flight updates.

Our departure time slowly changed to 10, then 11, 11:30, and finally midnight. We learned that the incoming flight had returned to its gate, darkened by a Nor'easter. New regulations limit the time airlines can keep their passengers sitting on the tarmac, and it had been three hours. The constant delays were a deception. I knew this plane was not going to make it to New York. The Buffalo crew had been in wait mode for over four hours. They were running out of time, and Delta wasn't going to call in a new crew at midnight. It was time to take action.

Although the gate attendant insisted that there was still a chance that the flight might not be cancelled, I called Delta Airlines. After an interminable wait, I was lucky to reach an accommodating agent. My timing was impeccable. Just as I was explaining the situation, I heard a mounting rumble among the other passengers who were following flight updates on their smartphones. Then came the official announcement: "Ladies and gentlemen, I regret to inform you that Flight 3287 to Raleigh-Durham has been cancelled due to inclement weather." People immediately scrambled to get in line to rebook their flights. I didn't have to push to the front this time. Providence intervened with my timely phone call. The three of us had a flight out the following morning.

Our combined advancing years obliterated any consideration of sleeping in the terminal like I did all those years ago when Air India launched my fear of flying. But what used to be the TWA terminal now housed comfortable queen-sized beds in a room with sound-proof windows. Its opening four days earlier was heralded in the press as a monument to a bygone era of flying, although still requiring work. Nancy booked a room on her cell phone. We grabbed our luggage and took the Air Train to terminal five, the home of the new TWA Hotel. We wheeled our bags through the iconic tunnel carpeted in red, glorified in Leonardo DiCaprio's *Catch Me If You Can*. By the time our heads met our pillows we had been traveling for over 24 hours.

The airlines still haven't broken me.

2

HEIGHTS AND ENCLOSED SPACES

I'm not afraid of heights. I just really respect them. That is why I stay away from the edge!

James Hauenstein

Phobias are not logical. I get uneasy in enclosed spaces, but not in an airplane, as long as there are windows, and there are always windows. I love windows. I hate that my therapist's office has no windows. I don't go to therapy to be entombed in a claustrophobic chamber. I ask her to keep the door ajar, despite the chance that someone might hear us. I have suggested she get a new office, but I am not going to leave her. It takes too long to break in a therapist, and I like her.

My travels have been undermined by two common phobias: claustrophobia and acrophobia, the fear of heights. On my European adventure in high school, Mr. Siegel, our art teacher, encouraged us to ascend the 387 steps up a winding staircase to the tower gallery of Notre Dame in Paris for a bird's-eye view of the grotesques and gargoyles protecting the Gothic cathedral. I picked up a brochure at the entrance that suggested the climb if we were "in fine fettle." I might have been in better shape at eighteen than sixty, but my fear of heights and enclosed spaces had already made themselves at home in my psyche. Still, having seen the 1939 film, *The Hunchback of Notre Dame*, with Charles Laughton, I imagined myself close-up with the cat-like creature with the long neck and gnarly teeth. I wanted to hug a gargoyle.

Timidly, I walked toward the stairway leading to the tower, only to be greeted by a warning sign: "Not recommended for people with heart trouble and women who are pregnant." I didn't have heart trouble, except for an annoying fluttering when I grew anxious. And I certainly wasn't pregnant. Nevertheless, the cautionary notice weakened my resolve, and, like the scaredy-cat I was, I decided to remain in the open nave instead.

As I turned my back on my two girlfriends who had already started their dash up to the tower, Felice turned around. "Where are you going?" she asked, before continuing her ascent. She and Karen were gone before I could make up an excuse for turning back.

It wasn't until my fourth visit to Notre Dame Cathedral in 1982 that I garnered enough bravado to hug the gargoyles. My then-husband Paul was my motivation. He agreed to join me on the trip because we had enough students for three chaperones to travel free, and my parents agreed to watch our son, Joshua, who was three-years old at the time. Leaving our student charges on their own to explore the City of Lights, we crossed the *Pont Notre Dame,* one of the many bridges spanning the Seine to *Île de la Cité.* We entered the square crowded with gawkers who didn't know where to look first: the two striking towers, the three delicately carved entrances, or the rose window with the spectacular colors gently muted by the sun. Paul was eager to climb the tower.

It's essential to understand Paul's quirks in order to grasp my willingness to confront my fear of heights and enclosed spaces and join him up the spiral staircase. He had little patience for weakness, whether physical or mental. He believed that, with a little self-discipline, we have full control of mind and body. For instance, after seeing a photo of himself with a bit of a belly as a result of keeping up with his pregnant wife's cravings, he was determined to eat a healthful diet and exercise. He hasn't deviated from that declaration in forty years. He runs, he bikes, and he swims. It's one of the many reasons he is my ex.

Determined not to reveal the extent of my anxiety, I asked him to walk in front of me so I could pace my climb. He bounded up the stairs with the confidence of seeing me at the top. As I scaled the very narrow, fan-shaped staircase, I became light-headed, followed by a tangible tingling around the crown of my head. It was as though my grey matter was sending electronic pulses from my skull to my skin. With no end in sight, I began to have more difficulty breathing.

Not only was I claustrophobic, but I was also out of shape. I was frantic to see a way out, a light in front of me. There was no exit, whether I looked up or down, so I tried to do neither. "Just keep looking at the stair in front of you," I kept telling myself. I tried counting the steps, but I kept losing my place.

By the time I made it to the summit of the South Tower, I had a faint ringing in my ear that was not emanating from the ancient Emmanuel bell in the tower, but from inside my brain. I leaned against the stone, waiting for my pulse to decelerate. I was grateful that Paul didn't find me until my heartbeat was almost back to normal.

"Are you okay?" he asked. I must have looked a little pale.

"I'm fine. I just walked up 387 steps, but I'm all right."

"Come take a picture." He waved me over to one of the chimeras sitting on the ledge of the tower wall. These creatures, unlike the gargoyles, were ugly decorative statues, like the evil cat that I remembered from the movie. Gargoyles, on the other hand, are purposeful: they act like gutters, draining the water away from the building.

I didn't want to get any closer to the edge. I had temporarily conquered the fear of enclosed spaces, but I was still afraid of heights.

"I can see from here. The view is fabulous," I lied. I couldn't really see much of Paris from where I was standing. Like when I was climbing the staircase, the secret to avoiding my fear of heights was to look out and not down. I staggered slowly over to the cat-like creature. Paul snapped a photo of me hugging the grotesque, while I attempted to smile, hanging on to the stone creature for dear life. We didn't stay long. Paul already had time to enjoy the view while he was waiting for me. Going down was much easier. All I had to do was remember that there was an exit, and I was almost there. It was a small, but important victory over my fear of heights and enclosed spaces.

A trip to Israel in 1996 also challenged me to confront both phobias. I was invited to join a group of Jewish camp directors on a FAM tour to preview a new program, appropriately termed *Etgar*, or "challenge" in English. FAM is a travel industry term for a familiarization tour, a chance for tour directors, travel agents, or, in this case, camp directors, to experience a program that they can sell to clients. In other words, we get to take a free trip.

When I told my mother about my opportunity to travel to Israel for a second time, she expressed considerable concern.

"You are not going," she insisted, even though she knew that I didn't have to listen to her now that I was a grown woman with two children.

Her apprehension was not totally unwarranted. Riots had broken out in Israel after the Hasmonaean Tunnels were opened to the public just a few months earlier. The entrance to the tunnels, which provide visitors with a glimpse of the underground sections of the Western Wall, originally stood in the Muslim Quarter of the Old City of Jerusalem. For days after the tunnels officially opened, members of the Israeli Defense Forces clashed with the Palestinian National Security Forces at the Western Wall tunnels. The uprising soon spread to Gaza and the West Bank. To make my mother even more nervous, earlier that year there were two terrorist attacks on the No. 18 buses in Jerusalem within days of each other, killing 45 people and injuring 48 more.

"It isn't safe. I will be worried about you the whole time. I prefer that you not go." She was in her anxious mother mode.

I tried to assuage her concerns. "Mommy, I have been to Israel before, and I never felt as safe. I will be fine."

"The last time you traveled to Israel people weren't dying in riots." She was right. 67 people had lost their lives following the opening of the tunnels. The peace talks between the Palestinians and Israelis had reached a crisis point.

Eventually, she relented. "If I can't stop you from going, can you at least promise me two things?" I guessed what she was going to ask.

"Please don't go near the tunnels and, please, do not ride the public buses."

I agreed, but, as it turned out, I lied.

Not quite as confident as I originally professed, I flew from National Airport to JFK a day before my departure to Israel so that I could see my parents — just in case the unthinkable happened. Before I left, my mother gave me a dollar for protection on my journey – the now familiar *Shaliach Mitzvah*. She was familiar with Jewish superstitions. I took my obligatory photo of our El Al plane for additional good luck. Being prepared for customs in Tel Aviv further reduced my anxiety. We left Ben Gurion Airport and traveled to Jerusalem to start our *Etgar* experience.

On our first morning, Ezra, our Israeli guide, walked us through Damascus Gate and into the Arab *shuk*, or market, in the Muslim Quarter of the Old City. When I first realized he was taking us to the tunnels, I felt the collywobbles, triggered by my mother's qualms as much as my claustrophobia. As we descended into the ancient Hasmonaean aqueduct, my concern about being caught in a political uprising vanished, but my dread of enclosed spaces increased. The dankness of the tunnels made me feel as though someone was stuffing a hot towel down my throat. As we followed Ezra through shadowy corridors and fragmented walkways, the inevitable tingling in my head ignited. I grabbed the nearest arm, and, as this now-forgotten camp director turned to me, she nodded in an affirmation of anxiety, and we started to sing a popular camp song alluding to Psalm 137 of the Torah:

By the rivers of Babylon, where we sat down
and there we wept, when we remember Zion.

Singing usually succeeds in distracting me. If I am reciting lyrics, I can't be contemplating getting trapped in an underground ancient passageway at the same time. However, I also can't focus on the fascinating facts the guide is revealing. We stopped singing in order to take heed of Ezra. I tried to control my breathing. In – one, two, three, four. Out – one, two, three, four, five, six. I can slow my heart rate by extending the exhalation, allowing me to listen to our learned guide.

"Where we are standing is actually a cistern, providing water to the Temple Mount during the time of King Herod. After the temple was destroyed by the Romans, they built right on top of the aqueduct."

I was relieved that only a small portion of the tunnels were open. Once we exited the passageways into the Armenian quarter, I was ecstatic to sense and sniff the fresh air, especially scented with the aroma of freshly baked breads. I wanted to buy one of the paper-thin sheets of lavash that had just come out of the *tonir*, or clay oven, smelling of wood-fire, but Ezra moved quickly through the crowded alleys.

I triumphed over my claustrophobia with a song and a helping hand, but later in the trip, I was assailed by acrophobia at the edge of the

Judaean Desert. Bordered by the Dead Sea to the east and the mountains of Judea to the west, the rough terrain of desert provided sanctuary to zealots like the Jews who inhabited Masada. The rugged cliffs were also home to Byzantine and Christian monasteries, most of which are in ruins. A handful, such as the Greek Orthodox St. George Monastery, are still extant. Also sacred to Christianity is the Jordan River, the site of Jesus's baptism by John the Baptist, which empties into the Dead Sea, the lowest elevation on our planet.

Earlier in the morning we had visited a spa in Ein Gedi, an oasis in the desert. I took a quick dip in the Dead Sea where the concentration of salt kept me afloat, but also stung the hell out of my recently shaven legs, thereby making it a very quick dip. Take note: do not shave before going into the Dead Sea. I next smeared my body with the requisite restorative mud bath and, allowing it to dry, I showered and changed, feeling rejuvenated. The sensation didn't last long, however, when I found myself standing with my peers in front of a row of jeeps in the Judaean Desert.

Everyone claimed a seat in one of the vehicles. Joining me in the jeep were our tour director, Ezra; Dava, the youngest of us and a consummate New Yorker; Stephanie, in her late thirties and hailing from somewhere in the middle of our country; and Jordan, a large bulk of a man from a camp in Houston, Texas. I was the fifth passenger, a middle-aged woman representing the Washington, D.C. camp. There was a professional driver guide at the wheel.

As the jeep descended the steep desert hills, I felt like an ice cube in a cocktail shaker. We were riding uphill over numerous valleys or *wadis*, from 1,300 feet below sea level to 2,600 feet above, and my bottom felt every bump. Dava hooted with excitement. Blonde-haired Stephanie, in pigtails to keep her long strands off her face, quietly endured the rough ride. Mustachioed Jordan played the rugged he-man without the body to match. For Ezra it was just another day at the office.

My anxiety started to surface when the jeep became perpendicular to the desert. I thought that one part of the Judaean Desert looked exactly like the sand we had just crossed. I closed my eyes and silently started counting backwards. It works to relax me the same way as singing.

Mercifully, the driver finally brought the jeep to a halt, and I opened my eyes to see that we had come to a bluff. Ezra suggested that we walk to the edge for a panoramic view of the Dead Sea and Jordan – the country, not our colleague. I happily stepped out of the jeep, relieved to be on somewhat firm ground. My feet froze in the sand as I watched everyone stride off with Ezra, like Moses leading the Israelites out of Jordan, although this time in the opposite direction. Stephanie turned back to see me planted firmly in the desert.

"Faye, aren't you coming?"

The edge looked precarious. What stopped the sand from swallowing me up as I fell down the embankment? What if I stepped too close, falling into the Dead Sea, even though it was miles away?

"No, it's okay. I can see from here," I said, in a familiar retort. I planted my feet in the desert sand, embarrassed by my fatuous fear of heights. With no conceivable excuse to offer, I stayed silent and waited for my fellow travelers to return from the abyss. As long as I didn't see the steep incline, I imagined that there was nothing dividing the horizon from the distant landscape

When my travel buddies returned from their brief adventure, I appreciated their considered refrain from mockery. I was paradoxically as happy to get back into the jeep as I was to get out of it. After four long hours over rock and sand, I soothed the collywobbles by downing a liter of water. I wished it was whiskey.

Five years later I was sans husband and both of my children were living on their own. I could travel anywhere and spend as much as I could almost afford. I went to Greece to commemorate the first anniversary of my divorce, which also happened to be my birthday. A year earlier Paul called to let me know he was able to get a court date for our divorce after a February snow delay.

"I have good news and bad news," he said.

"What?"

"Well, the good news is that we have a new date for the divorce."

"What's the bad news?"

"It's your birthday."

In a rare moment of spite, I answered: "That's a great birthday present!"

The following March, I was on a tour of Greece that included a four-days on the mainland through the Corinth Canal, to Delphi, Olympia, and Naphtali, followed by two days in Athens, concluding with a cruise of the Greek Islands aboard the *MTS Olympia Countess*.

On the last leg of my Greek adventure I decided to explore the islands on my own, unencumbered by the whims and needs of others. My solo expedition of Rhodes started at the Palace of the Grand Masters, built in the fourteenth century as a fortress, which also served as the seat for the Knight's Quarter. As I walked through the massive halls and great rooms, I was welcomed by a hooded crow or hoodie, with its grey body and black head, wings, and tail. The crow wasn't alone: a keeper held him on his forearm while gently petting its beak. I was enchanted, not by the hoodie, but by the Greek. His hair resembled that of the bird's, a pitch black with grey strands that didn't age him, but rather drew me to his chiseled face and olive skin. His blue-striped shirt was opened at the top, bearing a well-defined chest.

"This is our mascot."

"I'd like to take you home as my mascot," I thought to myself.

After a brief introduction to the fortress, the palace host invited me to enjoy my visit. It was time for me to stop daydreaming about the eye candy and to start exploring the palace. I meandered through the rooms of the building, most of which were renovated by the Italians after an explosion that destroyed much of the interior of the palace. Although the knight's armor and weapons held little interest to me, I enjoyed roaming through the rooms that were decorated with intricate mosaics of Greek mythology and Hellenistic designs that survived the explosion and the Italian redesign.

The gardens of the fortress contained a laddered entrance to the two and a half miles of ramparts that encircle the old city with views of its ancient edifices and verdant terrain. I walked confidently to the set of stairs that started perpendicular to the ground and then turned, parallel to the wall, reaching to the ramparts. However, as I climbed the first steps, I started to lose my conviction. I stopped, looked up and then down, and started to descend the three steps I had already conquered. I was glad that there was no one else making their way up to the ramparts so that I could keep my fear of heights to myself.

At the time I didn't see the irony that, despite being free from Paul, I was being held back by my own fears. I rationalized my retreat. I have so many other places I want to see. I only have the day here in Rhodes. The ship leaves before dinner. Quickly, I was back on the ground. I abandoned the towers and the cat walks. I was satisfied with the mosaics and a delicious Greek man with a bird.

I had traveled to Greece to celebrate my independence. Four years later I went to Texas to help my father overcome the loss of my mother. Travel always makes me feel better, so I thought the best way to brighten up my dad's days was to take a trip together. He wanted to see the Alamo, so we planned a visit to the Lone Star State, with stops in Austin and San Antonio. Traveling with my father forced me to slow my pace but added additional anxiety.

One of the most common hurdles for claustrophobics is the elevator. As soon as an elevator door shut me into the small vestibule, I felt as though the air was being sucked out of my lungs. I trudged up a staircase rather than enter a crowded lift. An empty one was just as fear-provoking because, if I became stuck in the elevator, I would be alone in my terror. I avoided this claustrophobic's nightmare until my father and I were departing Austin for our drive to San Antonio. Steps aren't a viable option when you and your 77-year old father are schlepping two large suitcases from your room on the eleventh floor of a hotel to check out.

After two nights in the luxurious Austin Hilton, my father and I stepped into the empty elevator for the last time. First, there was a bit of a jolt, and then it stopped. I took in a deep breath and looked over at my father who was remarkably calm. I pushed the red alarm button, considerably more times than necessary. Then I screamed: "Help!"

"Faye, you need to calm down."

"Daddy, I can't breathe."

"You'll be fine. But you have to stop screaming."

Between my screeching and button pushing, a voice from beyond responded: "Are you okay?"

"You have to get us out of here!"

"How many of you are in the elevator?"

"It's just me and my elderly father. He can't breathe. You have to get us out of here." My dad was breathing just fine. "He's 77, please, he can't stand for long." It was easier to use my father as an excuse rather than admit to my own claustrophobia.

"Okay, ma'am, but you will need to calm down." I heard that before. "We are going to try to start the elevator again."

We waited. Nothing.

I started to sweat, and, with an apology for the hackneyed phrase, the walls were closing in. "Is anyone there? Please, you have to get us out." My repetitious calls for assistance went unanswered.

"Faye, you are making it worse. You're scaring me."

Finally, I heard a voice from below. "I am sorry, ma'am, but we can't get the elevator started, and it is stuck between two floors. We have contacted the fire department. They will be here in minutes."

"Fuck. Fuck. Fuck. Fuck. Fuck," I cursed out loud.

I heard that swearing is good. Supposedly, it releases endorphins, increases your circulation, and can give you a sense of tranquility. It didn't work.

My dad, still composed, started to feel a little unsteady on his feet. I suggested that he lean on his suitcase for support. I stopped bellowing in deference to him, although when the fire department arrived I made sure they understood the depth of my anxiety.

A fireman took over the conversation. "We are going to turn off the power to the elevator and then turn it back on again. That often restarts it. You will feel a small jerk, but don't be concerned."

I thought to myself, "This is an elevator, not a computer. Is that really going to work?"

"Please," I pleaded loudly. "I have claustrophobia. I need to get out of this elevator." At least I started to accept responsibility for my bizarre behavior.

"That is exactly what we are doing, ma'am." I have never been called "ma'am" so many times in such a short period.

My father concurred with the fireman. "The fire department is here now. Your screaming isn't helping anything."

We heard a silence when the power was disconnected.

"Okay, now, we are going to turn the power back on. Are you ready?"

I had been ready for the last half an hour.

As soon as they switched the power on, the elevator shuddered and started to move. It wasn't until the doors opened to a sea of firemen and hotel staff that I took a deep breath. And then I started to cry. I am not sure if they were tears of relief, anger, or frustration.

One of the hotel managers handed a bottled water to my dad and me with an apology. I said thank you, but then I snipped: "You are lucky we weren't on our way to the airport." We were driving to San Antonio.

"Please come over to the desk. Let us take care of you."

We had reserved two rooms for three nights, and we had not yet checked out. I wondered if they might make the mishap worthwhile.

"We will take care of your rooms for last night." Two free rooms and two bottles of water in exchange for thirty frantic minutes in an elevator. It seemed fair to me, and we were off on the rest of our adventure, a little weary, but eager to remember the Alamo! Thankfully, it was the only time I have been stuck in an elevator.

Two years later, however, I was tricked into descending into the subterranean tunnels of Edinburgh. I was a solo traveler on a "Scottish Dream Tour" of the Highlands that included copious castles, verdant valleys, and an abundance of sheep. Our tour director, Richard, a professor of Scottish history, met us each day in full kilt regalia. His golden hair created a halo effect, and his matching eyebrows disappeared into his forehead. I mockingly called this trip "The Land of Sheep, Grass, and Castles," but it was a privilege to listen to Richard's extensive knowledge of his country, even if we had failed to unearth the Loch Ness monster on a visit to its lake home.

At the end of the escorted portion of the tour, I looked forward to getting out of the Highlands and discovering Scotland's capital on my own. After a day of sightseeing in Edinburgh, I returned to the hotel for a bit of a rest before dinner. As I walked into the lobby, I chanced upon one of the women who had traveled with me through the land of sheep, grass, and castles. Linda, who was accompanied on the tour by her husband, Terry, stopped me.

"How are you doing?" she inquired, before getting to her intended question.

After our cordialities, Linda asked if I might be interested in joining her that evening. "I really want to take a ghost tour in the Old City, but Terry is too tired and not very interested. I heard it's great. Any chance you might want to do that with me?"

When I heard "ghost tour," I didn't realize that a greater part of the experience was conducted in the subterranean caves below the streets of Edinburgh. Thinking that a night of ghost stories might be amusing, I agreed to meet her after dinner at the tour entrance on the main road of the Old Town. The instructions on the ticket said to meet at the blue phone box, one of the rare remaining old police stations or *tardis*. These served as miniature police stations where a local could make an emergency call in a time before everyone had phones. The fictional Dr. Who travels in his *tardis*, which transforms into a spacecraft that whizzes through time and space to solve the problems of the world. As I stood on the street wondering how something so small could become something so large, I was interrupted by Linda's arrival.

Following right behind Linda was a woman donning a black cape and carrying a lit candle, her blonde hair carefully tucked into her hood. She wore a red tag that assured us that she was a licensed guide. Our ghost tour began with a rather dreary visit through what was advertised as one of the most haunted cemeteries, Greyfriars Kirkyard, where our caped companion tried to frighten us with gruesome stories. She told us that the graveyard, which dates back to the 1560s, was plagued by body snatchers in the early 1800s. The corpses would be sold to the local medical school. Families erected iron cages, or mort safes, around the graves of their loved ones to protect them from falling victim to the ghoulish practice.

We didn't see any poltergeists. Upon exiting Greyfriars, we followed our guide down into the underground. "I ain't afraid of no ghosts," but I am categorically terrified of enclosed spaces.

There was no way out of the situation without embarrassing myself. As we descended into the charnel houses, the only light emanated from the caped guide's candle. I whispered to Linda.

"I can't do this."

"What's wrong?"

"I can't do caves. I feel like I am suffocating."

"Hold on to me."

Joining hands, Linda helped me navigate the seventeenth-century close, or alleyway, without having a heart attack. As we stepped into a couple of the rooms of the old houses that were supposedly inhabited by their otherworldly former residents, our mutely lit leader regaled us with stories of apparitions and ghouls. We paused in St. Mary's Close. I shut my eyes in an attempt to visualize myself in the open air while listening to the forlorn tale of wee abandoned Annie.

"Don't be frightened if you start to feel cold. There is an intense sensation of sickness in this room."

I assumed she was talking about me, still trying as hard as I could to imagine myself anywhere else.

"Watch out for a little girl named Annie. She has been known to reach out to visitors for help. A long, long time ago wee Annie was struck with the plague. Realizing there was no hope for their daughter, her parents did the unthinkable. In a horror we cannot imagine, they abandoned Annie here in the room, leaving her to die alone, with just a doll to keep her company."

Ironically, this pitiful story made me feel better. Concentrating on poor Annie allowed me to forget the oppressiveness of the underground city. I opened my eyes to discover a pile of dolls, among them Barbies, Raggedy-Anns, and baby dolls. A Japanese psychic first discovered poor Annie's anguish over her lost doll. In an attempt to appease the young spirit, the psychic, Aiko Gibo, left her a cloth doll made of a traditional tartan pattern. Following her lead, numerous visitors have added to Annie's collection. According to modern myth, as long as Annie has her dolls, her spirit is at peace.

My consideration of the dolls was interrupted by the ghostly tour guide. "As we exit into the evening, be careful, not only of the steps, but also of those spirits who may want you for company!"

Her hokey finish to the underground experience went unnoticed. I heard we were leaving. I grabbed Linda's hand again as we escaped the confines of the fetid labyrinth. Once outside, Linda dropped my hand and turned to me.

"Did you enjoy that?"

Was she being flippant? "No!" I answered, slowly elongating my voice like a cry of a ghost. "Well, I guess the first part of the tour was interesting – in the cemetery and the church – but the whole time we were underground all I thought about was getting out of there." I don't go too low down, and I don't go too high up.

The following year I gave in to my fear of heights on a business trip to St. Louis for an International Baccalaureate Heads of Schools Conference with my colleague, Linda. With time allowed for sightseeing, we plotted out the few things we wanted to see, do, and eat while in the city along the Mississippi, including the Gateway Arch, as well as the distinctly thin, square-cut round St. Louis pizza at Imo's with its Provel cheese, a delicious mixture of cheddar, provolone, and Swiss cheese.

The 63-story arch designed by Eero Saarinen, the same architect as the TWA terminal, commemorates the Western expansion of the country. It houses a museum in addition to the expansive views of St. Louis with a ride on a five-seater tram car to the top of the arch. The exhibit on the bottom floor included an original tram car from 1967 that, like the modern trams, swung like a Ferris wheel as it made its ascent to the observation deck near the top of the monument. The sign in front of the vintage car warned us that walking to the tram loading area at the bottom and then walking to the top requires going up and down several flights of stairs. Neither Linda nor I chose to travel up the arch, both victims of claustrophobia, acrophobia, and aging. We satisfied ourselves with a photo opportunity of a blast from the past.

A year later, however, I overcame my fear of heights walking on wobbly steel bridge across the roof of the rain forest in Costa Rica. I didn't conquer acrophobia: I just didn't allow it to stop me this time. I slowly put one foot in front of the other, placing one hand on the side of the bridge to keep me steady as I carefully maneuvered the hanging bridges of Mistico Park in Arenal. Pausing often to appreciate the dense forest and the abundant multi-colored birds, I was able to forget that I was high off the ground. Instead, it was as though I were walking on the top of the trees. If I could have seen the ground, I might not have been so daring.

None of the birds sat still long enough to snap a photo, but a quick glimpse of their colors was enchanting. I have minimal knowledge of our feathered friends, but I recognized a toucan with its colorful bill. It looked just like the bird on the Fruit Loops box, Toucan Sam, with the colors of the rainbow. Our tour director, Rolando, later told me it was most likely a keel-billed Toucan. I didn't sing nor count backwards; instead, I focused on the overpowering sounds, sights, and smells of the rain forest. Sometimes phobias win and sometimes I win.

3

FALLING

If there is a fear of falling, the only safety consists in deliberately jumping.

Carl Jung

Getting old stinks. Although I still think I'm young, my muscles and joints know differently. The fear of falling, or basophobia (literally, the fear of walking or standing erect) is a part of our survival system, especially in our later life when falls become more common. My phobia intensifies with age, triggering increased anxiety over my ability to manage cobblestone streets or steep inclines. That being said, I was only thirty when I suffered the worst fall of my life.

I fell in the most common place – my home. I was holding my three-month old daughter when, for no apparent reason, I stumbled, plummeting down the steep flight of townhouse stairs. My maternal instinct kicked in. Rather than attempting to stop my fall, I held Rachel securely in my arms. At the sound of the thud as we reached the bottom, Paul came running into the hallway to discover my ankle in a frighteningly unnatural position. He extracted Rachel from me before calling for help. He didn't dial 911. Instead, he called our next-door neighbors, Bobbie and George.

Paul and George tried to maneuver me into the back seat since the front of the car was out of the question. My ankle, now the size of a grapefruit, wouldn't bend into the required position to sit. Wincing at every move, I bit my tongue as the guys clumsily positioned my broken body into our small Toyota Corolla. In retrospect, it would have been safer if well-trained paramedics had lifted me into an ambulance. When the emergency room staff couldn't extract me from the car without causing unbearable pain, they chastised us for not calling 911. Eventually, an attendant grabbed the hem of my pants, pulling me in one direction while another took hold of my shoulders and pushed me through the open car door.

X-rays revealed that I had broken my ankle in three places. The orthopedist suggested surgery, using pins to reconnect my bones. As I began to dissolve in tears, I tendered a ridiculous argument.

"I can't. My daughter will starve!" Needless to say, that was an exaggeration. Rachel might not have taken a bottle up to that point, but she would eventually get hungry enough to accept a latex nipple.

I begged, "Please, aren't there any other options?"

"We could give you a local anesthetic and realign the bones manually. You will have to wear a full cast for six weeks followed by a walking cast for another six." I agreed to the long recovery because it would allow me to go home.

After anesthetizing my leg with Novocain, the orthopedist manipulated the ankle, assumingly able to realign the broken bones. The technician finished the job, wrapping my leg in plaster from a couple of inches below my groin to the point where my toes peaked out of the cast. I went home to nurse Rachel.

I wasn't afraid of falling before I did. But, as I reached middle age, my anxiety grew. My earliest memory of being irrationally afraid of plummeting down a mountain was on my first visit to Israel in 1993 when our group of Jewish educators visited Masada, a winter palace and fortification high on a mesa, built by King Herod over two thousand years ago. Surrounded by Roman troops in 73 CE, the fortress was the site of a mass suicide by Jewish zealots who had taken refuge on the plateau.

Like most visitors to Masada, we arrived before sunset. In order reach the fortification, we either had to walk up the Snake Path, with its 700 stone steps and gravel trail, or take a cable car to the top. I opted for the cable car. Surrounded by windows, I didn't feel claustrophobic in the relatively large tram during its three-minute ascent. I avoided acrophobia by looking straight out at the sunrise rather than up or down. The greater challenge came when the aerial tramway stopped, not quite at the summit. We exited the car on the side of the rock mountain, stepping on to a metal grate before climbing the rest of the way up the open steps.

I was petrified of falling, unable to convince my feet to take the first step on the final ascent to the fortification. The flimsy grill was not going to hold me. I tried to avoid looking down into the abyss. Starting to feel light-headed, I tightly grabbed on to the railing, but my legs were jiggling like Jell-O. One of my colleagues suggested I pose for a photo, distracting me from my anxiety. The photo of me in the Hebrew version of a red Coca Cola t-shirt belies my terror but corroborates my triumph.

After taking the picture, my friend Jill encouraged me to continue. "Don't look down. Keep focused on the next step." She offered her hand. I made it up to the ruins of Masada where, despite remaining at least two feet from the edge of the precipice, I learned about the 960 individuals who became martyrs, willing to die rather than become slaves or to be killed at the hands of the Romans. Suddenly and irrationally, I became very concerned about those people living on such a high precipice, ostensibly safe from their enemies, but in danger of falling. On the other hand, these were people who were willing to draw lots to kill each other until the last person committed suicide. I think they had enough on their minds not to worry about tumbling off the mountain.

Five years after I made the terrifying final ascent to Masada, the original 1971 tramway was replaced, now discharging visitors safely in a terminal at the summit. I haven't been back to Masada, but it's good to know that I won't have to totter along the metal grates if I ever return.

My anxiety about falling extends beyond myself. I suffer similar stress when I see someone else in danger of taking a tumble. Like my dad. After surviving being stuck in the elevator in Texas, we enjoyed the rest of our trip together, although I felt much safer once we returned the rental car that he insisted on driving. After a final night in a hotel at the Austin airport, we flew back to Washington National Airport where we planned on relaxing before he returned home to New York. Although the name of the D.C. airport was renamed to honor Ronald Reagan in 1998, we older residents, especially Democrats, refuse to acknowledge the change, so National it was.

Since I lived a short, one-stop Metro ride from the airport, I always took the train home. Although I had been anxious about taking the first step on to an escalator since I was a little girl, I became accustomed to them after moving across the street from the elevated Braddock Road station. Malcolm Gladwell suggests that it takes 10,000 hours of practice before becoming world-class at anything. I only needed about 1,000 escalator rides to be comfortable. I escorted my father and his large suitcase on to the metro in an unusual moment of fearlessness. After safely exiting the train, we walked over to the escalator to go down to street level, ignoring the elevator at the end of the platform. I suggested that my father get on the escalator first so that I could assist him, assuring that his bag was sitting on the step safely behind him.

As I placed my foot on a step a couple of rows behind his suitcase, I watched in horror as my father turned around to check his bag, only to lose his balance and go plummeting down the moving stairs. I couldn't catch him, so I screamed.

"Somebody, help my father!"

Just as his falling body reached the bottom of the escalator, a well-dressed woman in front of him turned around, grabbing his arm and lifting him up in time for him to step safely off the escalator with the suitcase a couple of steps behind him. Another commuter, a middle-aged suited gentleman, reached for my father's bag, preventing it from hitting him or anyone else. I was seconds behind, greatly relieved to find my father standing, body intact.

By that time, a Metro employee who had heard my bellowing rushed up to us, seeking assurances that my father wasn't hurt, mostly out of concern, but also in case of future litigation. He offered to file a report, but my dad refused, saying that, although he was a bit tousled, he was unscathed. As we started toward the exit, another well-dressed woman handed me her card.

"Please, I saw what happened. If you need anything please do not hesitate to call me." I looked down at the business card. "Lorraine Roberts, Esq. Washington Metropolitan Area Transit Authority. Legal Counsel." We never called, and I never took my father on an escalator again, except in my nightmares.

The following year I invited my dad to join me at a conference in Las Vegas. My mother and father used to love visiting Vegas to enjoy restrained gambling and unrestrained eating. I thought that my father could hang out in the casino while I was learning about updates and techniques for the Advanced Placement program. After the conference and about $200 in wins, we took an excursion to the Grand Canyon.

This time I didn't let my father drive. We took a Grey Line tour of the Hoover Dam and the West Rim of the Grand Canyon, which offers a distinctly more desert landscape than the more popular South Rim with its lush forest. As my dad and I exited the tour bus and walked toward the canyon, I was astounded, not only by the beauty, but by the lack of guard rails. We walked right up to the edge to look into the immense gorge. I wondered what was going to protect anyone from plunging into the ravine, including me, and in a second thought, my dad.

What rational person designed a vantage point without proper safety measures? I wasn't the only one who was scared to stroll too close to the edge. My father wasn't keen on getting a bird's-eye view either. We remained at a safe distance, but I didn't feel totally secure until we sat at a picnic table at a small nearby eatery with a view, my backside firmly planted on the bench.

My fear of falling into the Grand Canyon wasn't wholly irrational. Your chance of dying at the Grand Canyon is about 1 in 400,000, although dehydration and heat stroke are the more likely culprits than an accident. Still, people do fall – two or three people take the plunge to their death every year. Some of them are idiots taking a selfie.

After lunch we walked over to the Skywalk Bridge, which opened just four months before our visit. Built by the Hualapai Tribe, the bridge allows visitors to walk on glass, looking thousands of feet down into the canyon. For about forty dollars I could challenge my fears, strolling across the translucent horseshoe overpass with the gorge below. Needless to say, neither my father nor I handed over the money for a ticket to anxiety. As we watched the daring sightseers on the skywalk, we witnessed a middle-aged tourist on his hands and knees, crawling across the glass to the safety of terra firma, justifying our decision to stay on solid ground.

My tour guide colleagues make fun of their guests who arrive at the Grand Canyon, take a few photos, and promptly want to go to their next destination. Feeling a little guilty, I was, nevertheless, eager to leave when they called us back to the bus.

When I became a tour director in 2010 it meant that I had hundreds of additional people in my care who were in danger of falling. Niagara Falls was a favorite destination on my first tours. However, I worried about my guests falling over the ledge and plunging into the Niagara River. There were precedents for this. In 2011, a Japanese student did just that. The twenty-year old woman climbed over the railing at Table Rock, a plateau that juts out over the rushing waters of the Niagara River on the Canadian side. After climbing over the rail to get a selfie, she lost her balance on the slippery rocks. After her death by selfie, I recounted the cautionary tale on every visit to the falls. That frightened everyone away from the railing. However, I really need not have worried. Most everyone was over the age of sixty. Half of them had no idea how to take a selfie and most of them were unfit to climb over the rail.

Traveling with seniors often means somebody does fall. One of my guests took a bad tumble on a poorly lit path at the Jefferson Memorial. I didn't need a doctor to tell me she broke her arm since a bone was sticking out from her skin. On the first night in India, one of my fellow travelers tripped over broken concrete as we made our way to dinner on a crowded, neglected sidewalk in New Delhi, spraining his ankle and forcing him and his wife to return home. According to the Centers of Disease Control's website, one in four people over 65 falls each year. Many of those are in bathtubs.

On one of my last tours of the Eastern United States and Canada, I had just gotten under the covers of my very comfortable hotel bed in Quebec when the phone rang.

"Faye, this is Maureen. I am so sorry to bother you, but Judy's fallen in the tub, and she can't get up."

Echoing the renowned commercial for a medical alert, her voice played like a dream or a prank call. I crawled out of bed and turned on the lights to be sure I was awake. When I knocked on the hotel door of my two guests, Maureen answered, clearly relieved that assistance had arrived, but I wasn't going to be very helpful. Her 78-year old roommate had lost her balance in the bathtub and fell, trapping her right thigh under her backside. The open door to the bathroom revealed Judy stark naked in the tub. Since most people don't bathe in their clothes, I can't really explain my surprise. I think I did a good job of appearing nonchalant, as though seeing an elderly naked woman sitting on top of her leg in a bathtub was routine for my job.

"Can you help me up?" she pleaded.

"I am so sorry, but that is not a good idea. I might make it worse. I don't know if you have injured yourself, and I don't think I can safely pull you out. Maureen, could you please call the front desk and ask them to send an ambulance?"

As we waited for assistance, Maureen and I tried to ease Judy's distress, although neither of us thought of helping her put some clothes on. When the paramedics arrived, we were thankful that they spoke English since none of us knew French.

"First, why don't we get Mrs. Schmidt something to put on?" the young female paramedic suggested. She must have thought we were daft letting her sit naked, exposed to the cold.

"You were smart not to move her," the male paramedic added. At least we weren't totally incompetent.

The two paramedics assessed her situation, worried that her ensnared leg might be broken, or, at the very least, severely bruised. After a brief return to the ambulance to secure a wooden seat, the two paramedics lifted Judy up while I placed the portable chair under her. Together, they raised her in the seat and transferred her to the gurney for the short ride to the local hospital.

With Judy's encouragement, Maureen continued on the tour, hoping her roommate would catch up with us later. A week later, however, Judy flew back home to England, torn ligament and all. Consequently, in addition to being afraid of falling off a cliff, I became more anxious about taking a tumble in the shower. When I retired to a new house in North Carolina, I chose a pebble-stone floor to get solid footing in my shower, as well as a grab bar in the bathtub to make it easier to get in and out.

It's time to introduce my frequent travel partner, Susan. Globetrotting on my own dollar was expensive, especially when I couldn't finagle a free trip. When I was introduced to Susan, I found not only a good friend, but a gregarious, spirited travel buddy. Our mutual friend, Anita, thought us compatible because we were both single and both of us loved to travel. She wasn't wrong, even though we are quite different. By the time we took a road trip from Massachusetts to Maine, we had already been traveling together for five years.

Susan and I were staying in a bed and breakfast in Rockland, Maine, when she also fell victim to the slippery bathtub. The LimeRock Inn is an historic Victorian mansion, its green wooden exterior comple-mented by its purple double door at the entrance. The house, which has since changed owners, was filled with antique furnishings and modern amenities and two very nice gay men. The innkeepers, PJ and Frank, were exactly the type of people you want as your hosts: friendly, punctilious, and excellent cooks. At the recommendation of a fellow tour guide, we stopped overnight at the LimeRock Inn on the way to Bar Harbor from Portland. We were looking forward to one of the "best three-course breakfasts in all of Maine," according to the reviews.

Susan went into the bathroom to shower while I dressed. As I was blow-drying my hair, I thought I heard something fall over the noise of the dryer. I turned it off.

"Are you okay?"

She answered rather matter-of-factly, "No. I fell."

Thankfully, unlike my guest on the tour, Susan was able to get her-self up, sparing me from witnessing her nakedness. There is a limit to good friendship. She wrapped herself in a towel and walked out of the bathroom.

"Fuck." Susan and I have a similar vocabulary. "I really hurt my head."

I wasn't sure if she suffered any significant damage or if it was just something that would pass, so I suggested we go down for breakfast and see how she was doing after we enjoyed PJ and Frank's legendary repast. The guys greeted us at the entrance to the dining room only to be rebuked by Susan about the slipperiness of the tub and the lack of a bath mat. Concerned about Susan and, perhaps, a potential lawsuit, they insisted that we go to the local hospital. With the aroma of maple bacon and caramelized onions wafting from the kitchen, I reluctantly grabbed the keys to our rental car and drove Susan to what was little more than a clinic. I resented missing breakfast, but, after all, she was my best friend and isn't that what friends are for?

With no one else in the waiting room, Susan was quickly called inside where she was diagnosed with a likely concussion. The doctor told her that she was fine, but he advised her to take it easy the rest of the day. She did, however, have an awful headache.

PJ and Frank were delighted to see us on our return to the inn. Although we had missed breakfast, they cooked up a delicious meal of perfectly poached eggs, maple bacon, grilled potatoes, and blueberry muffins. As we readied for check-out, Frank promised Susan the purchase of bathmats for future guests and refused payment for the room. We were glad for their concern and grateful for their gesture.

Just months later, Susan and I were on a tour of Peru when we both fell victim to a fear of falling. While planning our trip, I found a horseback-riding excursion to the Maras Salt Mines in the Sacred Valley outside of Cusco that I suggested might be fun. Susan wasn't so sure.

She replied by email: "About the horseback riding. I just want to make sure that although we are going uphill, we are going uphill on ground not rocks ... that's my only concern. I have no problem riding a trail. I do not want to ride a rocky cliff. If that's the story, go ahead and book us. After all, if I can get you to sail on a deserted ship with two crazy killers, you can certainly get me to ride a cranky horse who will probably stop in the middle of our trip to take a dump (they always do)."

I booked the trip, which required the revelation of our weight to be sure we were under the 180-pound limit (each). We both made it, but by the skin of our teeth.

The Salineras Ride started at a ranch just outside the city of Urubamba in the Sacred Valley. Neither of us had ridden a horse in decades. After we received safety equipment and a brief riding lesson, the Peruvian Paso horses began the climb up the mountain along the bridle path, or *runañan*. The Peruvian Paso is known for its unique gait that creates a steady and stable ride, with two feet always on the ground. We rode up an ancient steep path, that was, to both of our dismay, along a rocky cliff. Neither of us felt secure, no matter how stable our horse might have been.

Although the scenery was mesmerizing, I was too afraid to look, fearful that the horse might take a wrong step to the left and fall down the cliff, with me on top of it. We were riding along the River Vilcanota, but it was far below us. All I was thinking as we climbed the mountain on our horses was what goes up, must come down. I had a bad case of the collywobbles, and Susan shared my anxiety.

I was thrilled when we finally arrived at the salt mines. I had a chance to appreciate the terraces comprised of about 4,500 salt wells created by the Incas, with walls of stone and mortar made of mud. It looked like a mosaic of white, brown, and cream-colored squares. After listening to our guide's brief commentary, Susan and I refused to ride back down. We didn't have the nerve. We spoke to our guide while the rest of our group was tasting the delicate pink crystal Maras salt.

"I am so sorry, but I am really scared," I admitted, although I am not sure why I was apologizing.

"What are you afraid of?"

"The horse might take one step in the wrong direction, taking me with it down the cliff."

"The horses are not stupid. They are not going to commit suicide."

Susan responded, more firmly and without apologizing: "I am not going back down. We told you when we booked that we were both beginners, and we were assured that the ride would be easy. I will be even more frightened going down, being able to see everything."

"Surely we can't be the only ones who can't make it back down?" I needed my anxiety to be corroborated.

"No, no one has ever refused to go back down."

"I can't believe that."

"I will need to call to have you driven back. There is a little café at the top, where we turn around, and you can sit there and wait for a ride."

We were relieved and willing to wait the hour. At least we knew we weren't going to fall off Qaqawiñay Hill.

And then there was the time that I fell flat on my face in the financial district of Manhattan, far away from any bathtub or cliff. The culprit was not a slippery surface, but a small step on the sidewalk. I was leading a theater tour of New York for one of my former students who taught English and Drama at a Christian school in Virginia. This was 2011, and Christie had graduated with the class of 1979. She had four adult children of her own and a grandchild on the way.

Our group of theater students had tickets for three Broadway shows and workshops. The itinerary also included a couple of walking tours, including Wall Street, Chinatown, Little Italy, and a visit to the National 9/11 Memorial.

Our guide for the walking tour of the downtown district had no sense of audience, let alone pacing. Despite my reminding Brian, a lanky, straggly-haired young man, that the students were from a conservative Christian school, he attempted to engage them with talk of alcohol and drugs. Twice warned by one of the parent chaperones to restrict his subject to New York history and culture, he must have thought whatever else he had to say wasn't important because he never stopped to be sure everyone heard him. The cold April wind was an additional distraction. The skyscrapers can work like a wind tunnel, producing strong gusts circling between the buildings. The kids were tired, cold, and bored. And I was frazzled.

Brian was guiding our group through Wall Street as though he were race walking. Despite the pleas to slow down, he kept a swift pace with me bringing up the rear, trying to keep the slowpokes, mostly chaperone moms, from getting separated. As Brian turned left and out of my view, I looked back to see if there were any stragglers behind me. Just as I turned, I missed a small step on the walkway, falling on my face. My glasses flew off, cutting the side of my nose, which took the brunt of the fall. I felt something fall out of my mouth. I assume I screamed, and three of the mothers at the back of the group ran to discover the cause the commotion.

As three chaperones made their way to my rescue, I spouted almost every curse word I knew, with apologies to the women. One of my good Samaritans was a former army medic, and a quick look at my nose convinced her it was broken. She also explained that I cracked my two front teeth, shearing them in half. It was my teeth that had fallen out of my mouth. I was living the nightmare I often had of my teeth falling out, a common dream associated with anxiety.

By this time, Christie made her way back to me, followed by her students and, finally, our tour guide. I held him responsible for my mishap. I briefly considered suing him for pain and suffering, as well as payment for my new teeth. I urged Christie and Brian to continue the tour while three of the chaperones remained with me. There was no reason for the kids to miss Chinatown.

One of the moms called 911 while another one held my shoulder, ducked down and whispered in my ear: "Do you mind if we pray for you?"

What was I supposed to answer? I figured it couldn't hurt, so I assented to the blessing. It wasn't the first time a Christian prayed for me.

They knew I was Jewish. It always comes up in New York, especially when I talk about the food—bagels and lox, black and white cookies, knishes, and egg creams. Nevertheless, the three women prayed: "Lord, we pray that our friend, Faye, be restored to health. You speak of healing and restoration, and we thank you for the miracles you perform today. We pray that her nose is not broken, and that she will soon be healed. Please reach down and surround our friend with peace and strength. We believe all things are possible. In the name of Jesus, Amen."

The situation was strangely surrealistic. I was sitting in the middle of a busy Manhattan corner, holding a handkerchief over my throbbing nose and covering my two broken front teeth, with three middle-aged women praying over me. The ambulance finally arrived, breaking up the prayer group. Kathy, one of the mothers, agreed to ride with me to the hospital while the other two caught up with the group. We were on our way to the New York Downtown Hospital, with its two-star rating.

The ER doctor assured me that the nose was not broken and that, of course, the teeth could be fixed by a good dentist. My face was already beginning to show signs of bruising, especially around the eyes and the nose, making me look as though I had been in some hell of a fight. Kathy and I still had time to catch a quick bite before the evening's show, so we took a taxi to the Jacobs Theatre to find a place to eat nearby. Since I wasn't quite up to eating, Kathy connected with her daughter, leaving me sitting on the steps of the stage door to wait for the return of Christie and the students to see the Broadway show, *Once.*

I tried to hide the broken teeth with a scarf that also served to protect my bruised face from the constant wind. My black eyes poked through the top, and I must have looked like someone had used me as a punching bag because a man driving a large black pickup truck stopped in front of the steps.

"Ma'am, are you all right? Do you need help?"

I looked to my left and then my right to be sure he was talking to me.

This was New York, a city with a reputation for being unfriendly and abrasive, and here was this strange man asking me if I needed help.

"No, thank you very much. I am just waiting for someone," as though that explained why I looked as though I were assaulted. He waved and continued driving down W. 45th Street. I called my sister Jeanne, who worked in a periodontist's office on Long Island, and asked if her boss could recommend a good dentist in Manhattan. She arranged for me to see a Park Avenue dentist the next morning.

The dentist bonded the two teeth with a type of resin matching the original tooth color. Before I went home, I almost looked normal. There was no lawsuit.

Five years later, I fell again, but this time I was walking alone, and it was slippery.

I was on small boat cruise of the east coast of the Adriatic from Split, Croatia, to Athens, Greece. I was traveling with two dear friends, Janet and Carolyn, not the same Carolyn as my early days of traveling, but a book club buddy. I had known Janet since before my daughter was born, but we had never traveled together. After the sudden passing of her husband, Janet asked me to be her travel buddy. It turned out that we were perfect partners. When I shared news of my impending trip with my book club, Carolyn was excited to sign up as well.

On the bus journey from Zagreb to pick up the ship in Split, we stopped for a visit to Plitvice National Park. The park consists of sixteen crystal lakes linked by cascading waterfalls, eventually tumbling into the Kozjak River. I was captivated by the grandeur of the lakes, reflecting a myriad of colors created by the diversity of minerals. Although we were well into the month of March, it had recently snowed; most of remaining snow was on the grassy area, but the walkways were slick.

Both of my travel partners were a little older than my 62 years. Neither of them thought she was able to handle the hike on the wooden foot-bridge that sits just inches above the water. Since the trail also includes slippery rocks and wetlands, Janet and Carolyn decided to stay safely back at the entrance. I was determined to go, so Janet encouraged me to borrow her walking stick. I agreed, thinking it might minimize my chance of falling.

Our group was walking the easiest trail along the lower lakes, beginning and ending at the entrance. Vasya, our Bosnian tour director, remained back with those who chose not to adventure further into the park. By the time I said my good-byes to the slackers, everyone else in the group had a head start, and I ventured out on my own.

The footbridge was a series of narrow pieces of wood that curved over the shallow water. The decking was uneven, with spaces between the planks. There was no railing. Distracted by the splendor of the waterfalls cascading over mossy rocks, I lost my balance on the slick surface. I struggled to steady myself with the walking stick, but, instead, I posited it right through a slot in the boards. My glasses flew into the water, followed by my small camera, which miraculously landed on a rock, unbroken. Somehow I managed to keep most of my body dry as I retrieved the glasses and camera from the lake. The sleeves of my top, as well as the bottom of my pants, were cold and wet, but I wasn't much worse for wear.

No one saw me fall. I managed to right myself, and, after determining that there were no broken bones, I dried myself off and continued the trek along the lake. When I finally made it back to the entrance, the last one to finish, I gladly returned the worthless walking stick to Janet. Walking sticks distribute your body weight, making it easier to balance, but you have to know what you are doing, and it takes practice. It also helps if you don't plant the pole in a hole.

It was about this time that my previously broken ankle started showing wear and tear. The arthritis was worsening, and the daily ten-mile walks on student tours in D.C. and New York were aggravating the weakened joints. Eventually, I had to give up guiding. Since it was getting too difficult to walk, I decided to move away from urban life and retire to an active adult community in Durham, North Carolina, home to Duke University and some of the best orthopedic surgeons in the world. My doctor and I were exploring options before scheduling surgery when I took Rachel on a pre-wedding trip to South Africa. It was January, and she was getting married that June.

On a quiet Sunday afternoon in Cape Town, Rachel and I were walking down an abandoned street looking for something to eat. After an unsuccessful search for an open restaurant, my ankle, scarred and inflamed, decided it didn't want to walk anymore. The pain was unbearable. There was no sign of a taxi, and we didn't have an international phone to call Lyft or Uber or the local *Ola* or *Didi*. Rachel started walking toward a more populated street, with me following as best I could, until we reached signs of activity, where we were able to hail a taxi back to the hotel.

When I arrived back in Durham, I returned to my renown orthopedic surgeon and agreed to be a guinea pig for a new ankle system he and his partner had developed. He implanted a molded polyethylene bionic ankle along with innumerable pins and screws to allow me to continue to satisfy my compulsion to travel. He also fused my heel to decrease the arthritic pain in the joint beneath the ankle. A month later I was scurrying around on a knee scooter. Two months after that, still in a walking boot, I was leading my community's travel club on a trip to Charleston, even though I had to rely on pedicabs and taxis. Obsessed with travel, I am not going to let a little thing like falling stop me.

4

MEN

Sometimes I wonder if men and women really suit each other. Perhaps they should live next door to each other and just visit now and then.
Katherine Hepburn

Basta. According to my high school teachers, it was the most important word I needed in Italy. It means "enough," a clue for the Italian men to leave us alone. I was boy crazy in middle school. I did my fair share of making out at Bar Mitzvahs. In high school I was attracted to guys that garnered disapproval from my parents because their last names were Treglia and Bellavita, not Goldberg or Friedman. I married the first Jewish boy I dated. Before Paul formerly asked me to marry him, my parents booked a catering hall for our wedding. Less than a month before the ceremony, I began to think I was making a mistake, but I was too embarrassed to call it off.

I have had a conflicting relationship with men: I want one, but I don't like most of them. Men have brought both anxiety and joy to my travels, starting with that first trip to Europe as a senior in high school with two of my boy-crazy friends. Karen and Felice regarded our journey as a philanderous quest. They had no need for our chaperone's warning that we were in danger of being followed by strikingly handsome Italian men. I went along with my coquettish friends, but my acute sense of anxiety and painful shyness kept me at a distance.

Our first evening in Rome was our first night on the prowl. We heard that the Spanish Steps, a steep set of stairs joining the *Piazza di Spagna* and the *Piazza Trinita dei Monti*, with its iconic church at its pinnacle, was the place to go, not for its historical or cultural significance, but because we surmised it's where the hip people hung out. Hoping to become a muse to a man, women have been lured to the steps for centuries.

We were not handsome women. Felice was adorable, with eyes that always looked like they were smiling. She was petite, and barely seventeen. She flirted her way into the hearts of many boys. As Tommy's chatty New York girlfriend in our school production of *Brigadoon*, Felice fit right into the seductive role. Karen towered above Felice and boasted a raucous laugh that made others grin. Although diminutive, I still had about an inch or so over Felice, but I didn't have her endearing smile or her charming wit, and I didn't have Karen's engaging humor. I wasn't very sociable nor funny when I was in high school.

Filled with assurance, Felice and Karen were determined to track down handsome Italian men, with me tagging along, each of us oblivious of the extraordinary Baroque water fountain. The marble stairs were jam-packed with people: long-haired American college students in t-shirts and jeans perched next to swarthy Italian men, some of whom could have been our grandfathers. It was still early by Italian standards, with the sun just beginning to hide behind the church. As it began to set, sophisticated long-legged women with olive skin merged with the crowd. Karen and Felice were undaunted. Picking up young Italian men on the Spanish Steps both frightened and thrilled me, but I was content to be a bystander.

As we settled ourselves in the center of the plaza, our eyes simultaneously scrutinized the gathering of tourists and locals. Felice spotted two young men in their early twenties surveying the crowd as well. When the shorter of the two regarded the glimmer in Felice's eyes, she followed up with a coy smile and a flirtatious wink. She nudged Karen, who noticed the taller Italian turning to her at the same time. His reflection spoke of appreciation and attentiveness. Sitting only steps up from them, we tentatively waved an invitation for them to join us.

There was no doubt that we were American teenagers. Their "*buona sera*" was quickly followed by "hello." The taller one asked for confirmation. "You are American, no?" Felice quickly replied with a buoyant affirmation.

"*Voi regazze siete bella.* My name is Francesco." Felice giggled. She knew that *bella* meant beautiful, so she rightfully assumed he was complimenting her. "My name is Felice. This is Karen and Faye."

Francesco threw a flirtatious smile at us as the second Italian continued with an introduction, a little more confident in his English. "My name is Paolo." I remember Paolo's brown hair with its curls and lighter color. It didn't match my stereotype of the Italian man. Francesco's thick black mane and olive complexion were a cliché.

A language barrier didn't prevent Felice from pairing off with Francesco while Paolo made his move for Karen. I am assuming my girlfriends' flirtations, on top of my discernible caution, contributed more to the men's choice of girls than our looks. I wasn't unattractive. Although I was left out of the ensuing canoodling, I really didn't mind. I was content to sit on the historic steps and observe the swarm of people, sheltered from the seductive *maschi.* "When evening comes the heart unchains itself," according to the Italian song, "*I Maschi,*" or "The Men." The game of pick-up became a spectator sport for me.

Eventually, I tired of watching the public make-out party. I looked down at my watch, noticing the late time. Always the good girl, I didn't think missing curfew on our first night in Europe was smart. After a little coaxing from me, we left the guys on the steps and walked back to our dismal student hotel. For three Long Island high school girls, the evening was our idea of a grand European adventure.

The last night of our school trip had a similar plot. We decided to throw caution to the wind, not that we were guarded in our earlier exploits. The three of us walked to the western edge of the 16th *arrondissement* of Paris to the *Bois de Boulogne.* There, between the gardens and the lakes, we stalked young Parisian men. It wasn't long before we met two handsome young *hommes* walking the same path. We flirted, and, again, I willingly stepped back. The winding walkway of the *Jardin d'Acclimation* was lined with benches, a perfect spot for two titillated teenage girls to make out with Frenchmen. The couples each claimed a park bench, and, while I was secreted behind a tree, they had quite an arousing tryst. I wasn't disappointed to spend my last night in Europe watching my best friends: I was living prudently and vicariously.

Four years later I would be married. To say that Paul and I got off to a rough start would be an understatement. My lack of appreciation for money frustrated Paul. He saved and I spent. Unfortunately for me, travel was not on his radar: "Where are we going to get the money?" However, I was determined to find a way to travel despite a lack of funds and a husband with little interest in doing so.

I was elated to soon discover that I could indulge my wanderlust with free international trips simply by signing up a group of students with an educational tour operator. Over the years I traveled with students to Italy, England, France, Germany, Switzerland, Belgium, Austria, Liechtenstein, and the Netherlands.

I was traveling with my friend and colleague, Carolyn, and my sister Reneé, on our second trip to Europe with students. Our Austrian tour director, Norman, with his dirty blonde curls and boyish face, melted the hearts of all the girls. On the other hand, Wolfgang, our bus driver, could have stepped right into the role of a German *commandant*. His harsh features were amplified by his guttural German. As far as I knew, he didn't speak English. By the time we reached the university city of Heidelberg, Carolyn, a few years out of a dreadful marriage, and Norman were exchanging amorous glances.

With our students settled into their hotel rooms on our one evening in Heidelberg, Carolyn, Norman, Wolfgang and I took a walk to a local watering hole. It was more like a double date than four *bier trinken* companions. After a brief, three-sided conversation, Wolfgang turned to me with his wallet open, abruptly flashing photographs of children whom I assumed were his. By then, Carolyn and Norman disappeared on to the small, crowded dance floor, entangled in a flirtatious gambol.

Without warning, Wolfgang turned to me and announced: "You are welcome in my bed tonight," in clear, perfect English. I wondered if his parade of pictures of his kids constituted foreplay.

Dumbfounded, I turned to him and replied, "No, thank you."

Meanwhile, Carolyn and Norman were engrossed in a coy series of dance moves. I ordered and downed another drink before excusing myself to Wolfgang, begging fatigue and justifying my rudeness with the fact that I had a husband at home. Forsaking the paramours, I abandoned Wolfgang and absconded drunkenly into the streets of Heidelberg.

I was a little more than tipsy. On my way back to the hotel, I felt as though the sidewalks grew rather narrow. I meandered without direction, making it an interminable walk back. I began to sing softly to myself.

It could be so exciting, to be out in the world, to be free!
My heart should be wildly rejoicing, oh, what's the matter with me?
I've always longed for adventure, to do the things, I never dared.
Now here I am facing adventure, then why am I so scared?

Songs from musicals like *The Sound of Music* are on the playlist of my life.

I struggled to stay on the pavement, stumbling into the road throughout my intoxicated expedition. When I finally tracked down our small tourist hotel on Hauptstrasse, I made my way back to my room, threw myself on the bed and simultaneously cried and laughed in relief, not thinking to lock the door. About an hour later, I was awakened from my drunken stupor to find a middle-aged stranger in his underwear standing by my bed and Carolyn nowhere to be found. He stood over me as though it were a natural occurrence to walk into someone's room in one's tighty whiteys.

Looking straight at me, he asked in broken English, "You got fire for me?" Fortuitously, just as I was reaching for words, Carolyn walked in, calmly shooing our unwanted guest out of the room and locking the door behind him. As soon as she latched the safety chain, we heard his familiar bellowing: "You've got fire for me? You've got fire for me?"

Without any sense of irony, Carolyn answered, "No, we are too tired!" To my relief, he simply walked away.

I shunned the Italian and Parisian men, my bus driver, and the man in his underwear, but, when Paul and I went to Savannah to celebrate our twenty-fifth anniversary, I was hoping for romance and a chance to reconnect with the man. Even though Paul wasn't particularly interested in travel, he acquiesced to my suggestion to go to Savannah because he had loved John Berendt's *Midnight in the Garden of Good and Evil*, a mystery set in this city of verdant squares and antebellum mansions.

Unfortunately, when we planned our trip for March, we were oblivious to the fact that the city turns into a three-day celebration of St. Patrick's Day, especially along River Street. Our hotel, the historic

Planters Inn on Reynolds Square, was a block from the waterfront celebration.

The official St. Patrick's celebration started on Friday. Luckily, we had signed up for the "Midnight in the Garden of Good and Evil" tour for the day, exploring sites from the book, including Mercer House and Bonaventure Cemetery and keeping us away from the St. Patrick's Day events. A tourist van picked us up at the welcome center and made its first stop at Mercer House on Monterey Square, where antique dealer Jim Williams held lavish Christmas parties. It was here that Williams was arrested for killing his secret lover, Billy Hanson, shot dead in the early morning of May 2, 1981. The red-brick home, still owned by the Williams family, wasn't open to the public until four years after Paul and I visited, so we had to be satisfied looking through the wrought-iron fence of the 1868 home built for Confederate General Hugh Mercer, great-grandfather of the famous singer, Johnny Mercer.

After learning about the trial and the other colorful characters in the story, including my favorite, Lady Chablis, we ended our tour in Bonaventure Cemetery, site of the Bird Girl Statue whose photo adorns John Berendt's book cover. The young girl's head has a slight tilt to the left as she looks forlornly forward, two bowls in either hand. One of several castings, the bronze statue, renamed "Little Wendy," adorns a family plot in the Savannah cemetery. Our tour guide failed to tell us that the statue that Jack Leigh photographed had been moved to the Telfair Museum in 1997. We were looking at a cheap copy.

Both of us enjoyed our tour, having loved the book and the subsequent movie with Kevin Spacey as Jim Williams. Tired from the day's sightseeing, we both went to bed early. Unfortunately, the growing commotion outside kept us awake. The loud music was almost drowned out by boisterous drunken shouting and laughter. I might have been able to fall asleep if Paul hadn't been so cantankerous.

"What the hell? I can't stay here. How the hell are we supposed to sleep?"

I tried to mitigate the noise by suggesting pleasant background music in the room.

"We're going home."

"What are you talking about?"

"I am going to call the airlines and get us a flight tonight." It was probably around 8:30. Paul was an early-to-bed, early-to-rise person, and I had nothing better to do than follow him to sleep.

"That's ridiculous," I said, not helping the situation.

He called Delta anyway. There were no flights out that night and none available the next day, at least none without paying a high change fee, and Paul was too cheap for that.

I said, "Look, the St. Patrick's festival is over tonight. Tomorrow should be quiet, and we can enjoy our last day." The grumbling continued for a while until, exhausted, we both finally fell asleep.

The journey home a day later did nothing to ameliorate our stressful trip. The flight from Savannah to Atlanta was delayed, generating a run from one terminal to another to catch our flight to National Airport. Paul, who ran an hour every day because he enjoyed it, suggested we outrun the Plane Train that transports passengers between terminals. Maybe he was able to run, but I was out of breath within seconds. I ignored him and hopped on the train while he forged ahead on foot.

Paul made it to the gate minutes before I did. The agent was about to close the flight, prompting Paul to shout at me to run faster. With me in obvious physical distress, the agent was kind enough to keep the door open for boarding. Once the gate door closes, there is no getting in. The door was closing on our marriage as well. Five months later we agreed to separate. After a failed marriage and ten years of disastrous dating, I declared to myself: "*Basta!*"

I never traveled with Paul again. My next, and last trip with a man, was not long after we separated. I met Elliot on JDate, a site for single Jewish people looking for love and companionship. I should have run in the other direction when I discovered that Elliot was a momma's boy. But, instead, I lured him into my travel obsession. We made plans for a trip to New Orleans. A couple of weeks before our departure I realized there was no chance for us to develop into a meaningful relationship. Yet, following an unhealthy pattern, I didn't break up with him. Instead, I reasoned that since Elliot had already paid for the trip, why not go and enjoy our adventure at his expense, and then I'll ditch him. Wanderlust generates imprudent decisions.

The trip did nothing to assuage my dislike of Elliot, nor men in general. My assessment that our relationship was doomed was justified in the first hours after our arrival. We were staying in a delightful bed and breakfast in the Faubourg Marigny neighborhood, the NOLA gay district. Elliot didn't notice the rainbow flag at the entrance to our B&B. It wasn't until we were walking toward Bourbon Street that he asked why so many of the bars and restaurants were flying rainbow-colored banners. Elliot lived just miles from Dupont Circle, the gay center of D.C. How could be so clueless?

We decided to unpack before dinner.

"I can't remember the combination on the suitcase lock," he said.

"You probably picked numbers that mean something to you."

"It's my daughter's suitcase. I found it up in the attic, and it's in better shape than mine, so I decided to bring hers instead."

"Well, then, it's probably a number that was important to her."

"Yes, I am sure it is her birthday, but I can't remember it."

I might be judgmental, but what father doesn't remember his daughter's birthday? Better yet, what father choses his mother over his daughter and granddaughter? I knew that Elliot was estranged from his daughter. After his daughter had an out-of-wedlock baby from an interracial relationship, Elliot's mother gave him a choice – her or his daughter. He chose his mother.

What the fuck was I doing traveling with this man? We were going to be in New Orleans for two more days, and I wasn't sure how I was going to get through it. The answer soon became obvious. What else does one do in New Orleans than drink? What better way to keep sane with this man than being smashed the whole time? And that is what I did.

I was on a roll when I discovered alcoholic drinks at concession stands on the street. That evening, on our way back to the bed and breakfast, I had to pee so badly that I was afraid I wouldn't be able to hold it in until we returned to our room. As we walked through the residential neighborhood on our way back to the B&B, I was on the verge of public indecency. Stopping in front of a darkened home, I announced that I was just going to squat right there. Elliot was having none of that. He grabbed my arm, holding me up until we made it back in time. When you have the go to the bathroom that badly, finally being able to relieve yourself is ecstasy.

After three blurry days of eating fabulous food, visiting local sites, and drinking to oblivion, we flew home, but not before I told him that our relationship was not going to work out. I am more transparent than I realize. Despite my attempt to keep my feelings from him, he knew better. By the third day he was badgering me to confess the reason for my scorn. I did. The last time I saw him was when I said good-bye at the airport.

Except for my father, I never traveled with a man again. But I learned a new way to enjoy men from a distance: Susan's man of the day. Her ritual search for a good-looking guy each day of our journey began soon after we started traveling together. Susan is a notable flirt, but unlike Karen and Felice, she isn't interested in public displays of affection or a one-night stand. She just wants to put her arm around a cute man and take a photo to share with her Facebook friends who anxiously wait to see her man of the day. As usual, I stay in the background.

It begins with a stake-out. She eyes the men in restaurants, museums, or just strolling the city. "Look at him. He's a good man of the day!" Curiously, I don't see a type. He is often cute, or perhaps handsome in a rugged way, but sometimes not. He might have a sweet smile or beautiful eyes. Sometimes she doesn't declare him to be the man of the day until he speaks, uttering an accent that makes both of us swoon. The funny thing is that he is always flattered. Every man she has chosen has agreed to take a picture with her. Sometimes they have asked for her name so that they can friend her on Facebook and brag about being chosen. Susan's "man of the day" has led both of us to uncanny close encounters.

One of our overseas adventures took us to the small Central American country of Panama. There was no question that Susan's first man of the day would be our tour director, Carlos. His youthful face was topped with dark curls. His eyes, although small and dark, peered right into you. Carlos was delighted to take part in the ritual. He wrapped his large arms around Susan, grasping her hands in his and, thus, joined the other men who populate Susan's Facebook page.

By the next morning one of our friends back home replied to Susan's post: "OMG…I think I know him. Did he used to work on a cruise ship? If so, I'm 99.9% sure it's the same guy. He was my waiter on Princess, and he sent me flowers. We kept in touch for a long time, and we met for lunch one time in Florida when he was in port. I have pictures!"

A follow-up email revealed that the long-distance relationship was too difficult and, thus, Melanie and Carlos parted far-flung friends. Since that time, Carlos had married and was a father to two young children. Susan and I were both anxious to tell Carlos the news: we had a secret.

Usually when we entered the dining room for breakfast, Carlos sat at the front table, ready to greet his guests with a smile. However, this morning, impatient to share our discovery, we found no sign of him. After gathering our breakfast from the buffet, we kept our eyes out for him as we ate deep-fried corn tortillas heaped with scrambled eggs and bacon.

When we leapt from our seats as he entered the room, he must have thought we were nuts. At first we tripped over each other in an attempt to share the news, but I acquiesced to Susan: after all, he was her "man of the day." His boyish, round face opened up with a smile that revealed his disbelief and delight. "NO…no…really?" We showed him the proof—a picture of the two of them that Melanie sent us—and he surprisingly reacted with a request for her phone number, dialing it at once. Quietly, Carlos retired outside to finish his call, more so to get away from the din of the breakfast conversations than for privacy. After a chance to catch up on the years, he returned with a bear hug of appreciation.

There were many men of the day before and after Carlos. There was the rough-shaven fisherman at Seattle's Pike Place Fish Market whose encounter included the throwing of fish. There was the captain of the small tourist boat in Portugal whom I mistook for a rapist and killer. There had been a lot of waiters. Panama's Jose was one of my favorites. Susan called him "adorable" on her post. It was a fitting description since he looked as though he might be eighteen. A friend suggested that Jose looked just like a young Orlando Bloom. Although Susan's innocuous love of men permitted her to rob the cradle, she admired both the young and the old.

Our trip to the Northwest United States included a couple of days in Portland, Oregon, where we had a second "one-degree of separation" experience with Susan's "man of the day." A shopping jaunt took us to a small store called The Meadow. Filled with hand-crafted chocolates, gourmet salts, and crafted cocktail bitters, the shop found fame after its owner, Mark Bitterman, wrote a book about salt—*Salted: A Manifesto on the World's Most Essential Mineral*, although not exactly leisure reading. We met a young clerk in Bitterman's store. I have forgotten the name of this "man-of-the-day," but I remember his head of hair reminded me of George Clooney in his early days. He had a well-manicured beard and a smirk that indicated that he thought both of us a bit peculiar. However, like the other men, he granted Susan's request.

A couple of hours later, Susan's phone dinged with a text. "OMG!..." Bombshell posts somehow evoke a response of "Oh, my God!" The text continued: "Are you in Portland? That's my boss...that is my store where I work." In a six-degrees of separation paragon, Susan's man-of-the-day was her former roommate's boss.

Ondreya, a twenty-something flight attendant, had rented the loft in Susan's condominium when she was based out of Dulles Airport in Virginia. They had lost track of each other, and in that time, Ondreya had moved to the West Coast. A couple of phone calls later, we had plans to meet her and her boyfriend, Jared, at a local restaurant where he was part of the wait staff. We dined on fresh pasta and seafood from a Mediterranean-inspired menu served by Ondreya's endearing beau, who also picked up the tab. Susan didn't waste the opportunity to grab Jared as her "man of the day."

Susan's man of the day is fun. It's relatively safe – at least we haven't encountered anyone who threatened us. Susan usually flirts with the guy before making any declaration of intent. There is no attachment, no troublesome relationship, no annoying man with whom to travel. We leave him just where we found him.

Right before my first solo trip, I read an article about travel and men: "The most important point to remember is that a trip is doomed to failure if its primary goal is to find romance." I saved the newspaper clipping as a reminder in the very unlikely case that I ever travel in search for love.

5

PENISES

*It had a sort of a head on it, like a mushroom, and its color was red-
dish purple. It looked blunt and stupid, compared, say, to fingers and
toes with their intelligent expressiveness, or even an elbow or a knee.*
Alice Munro, *Lives of Girls and Women*

The first time I saw a penis was on my high school trip to Europe. It was
hanging on the legendary statue of Michelangelo's *David* at the Acca-
demia Gallery in Florence, Italy. Although my friends and I attempted
to feign a mature demeanor, we giggled over the curves and sinews of
David's marble body. My first impression was that David's penis was
awfully small, but I was clever enough to understand that it was in a
flaccid state. We were wandering around the museum without a teacher
or guide to inform us that Michelangelo painted the young shepherd as
he was about to confront the giant Goliath, not on a sexual exploit.

Although relatively naïve when it came to the male body, I recognized
that King David wasn't circumcised, despite the fact that he was a Jew.
David's father, Jesse, would have certainly followed God's commandment
to Abraham: "Every male among you shall be circumcised. You shall
circumcise the flesh of your foreskin, and that shall be the sign of the
covenant between me and you. At the age of eight days, every male among
you throughout the generations shall be circumcised." (Genesis 17)

Michelangelo, however, wasn't concerned with authenticity. He
sculpted David in the Greek tradition with the foreskin intact. In addition,
Michelangelo's model was most likely an uncircumcised Italian youth.
Without any further evidence, I decided that the circumcised penis was

more appealing. I saw my first live penis not long after our encounter with David, and it was circumcised. I still thought it rather ugly and unruly.

On my second trip to Europe I was a more mature, married woman. Carolyn and I walked our students to a small corner in Brussels to see the Manneken Pis, a statue of a naked boy whose piddle forms a small waterfall from which 17th century Brusselaars drank. Many of us were surprised by its diminutive size, not of the young boy's penis, but of the bronze statue of the boy standing atop the rococo fountain and peeing into the stone basin. We came upon the Manneken Pis in his birthday suit, although he owns a closet full of clothing. Legend has it that the peeing boy was caught in a witch's spell, frozen forever as punishment for urinating on her door. Or perhaps he saved all of Brussels from fire by defusing an explosive with his tinkle. I was just as delighted by the little pissing boy as my students, envious of his ability to stand and take aim.

Many of the statues of the male Greek gods and other choice men, such as warriors and athletes, would have trouble taking aim since their members have been lost to time. If their penises had still been attached, they would have been small like Michelangelo's *David*. I was reminded of my first penis sighting on a tour of the Archaeological Museum in Athens. Like David, the extant phalluses were flaccid. Our tour guide, Dorina, in her ridiculously high heels, told us that a statue of a god was distinguished from a statue of a mere mortal by the size of his penis: the smaller size of the omnipotent god reflected the Greek sensibility of authority and intellect. Although many of the statues were sans phallus, I didn't see much difference between the gods and the men who still had one. A champion athlete lacked his member, but, from what was remaining, I imagined his penis, like those of the gods, reflected his strength in its small size.

On a visit to the museum a decade later, I realized that Dorina had misspoken. The difference in size was not between mortal man and the gods, but between good and evil. The lustful, depraved satyrs brandished erect penises that were two or three times the size of an average man's. These were most evident in the illustrated pottery whose scenes also included drunken parties, prostitutes, and orgies. Not only did I not envy such a penis, I couldn't imagine the pain it would cause.

The ancient pottery also revealed the Greek preference for a foreskin that not only covered a flaccid member, but also one in an erect state. I had learned in grade school that Greek men engaged in athletic feats and fierce battles stark naked. I remember tittering at the thought of the first Olympians in their birthday suits. However naked they were, the men still considered it immodest to expose the glans. In order to hide the head of the penis, the *akroposthion*, or the tip of the foreskin that extends beyond the glans, was tied up with a thin, leather strap or cord called the *kynodesme*, the ancient Greek equivalent to a cock sock.

On a visit to the National Museum of Archeology in Athens a guide pointed out an ancient cock sock on a *lekythos*, an ancient Greek vessel that was used for storing oil. I moved closer to the pottery to see the male youth being chased by two *erotes*, winged gods of love and sexual intercourse. The gods attempt to grab the youth whose penis is clearly tied together, hiding the glans. I still prefer the circumcised look. Forgetting any current social and ethical trends against circumcision, I think removing the foreskin to expose the head is aesthetically pleasing.

I read the canon of Greek plays as a drama major in college, and I always wanted to stand in the Theatre of Dionysus, where the great tragedies like *Oedipus* were first performed. The comedies were just as remarkable. Aristophanes wrote much about "pricks" in his social comedies. I particularly appreciated *Lysistrata*, where the women withheld sex until the men stopped fighting. The actors who played the licentious men donned erect penises as part of their costume. In another comedy, *The Clouds*, Aristophanes corroborates the accepted perspective about size. The personified character of Just Cause describes the ideal traits of a man: "a gleaming chest, bright skin, broad shoulders, tiny tongue, strong buttocks, and a little prick." I'm for all of them, except the last one.

In his 1974 stream-of-consciousness novel, *Something Happened*, Joseph Heller's narrator declares that Freud was wrong about penis envy. "Women don't suffer from penis envy. Men do."

Early in my career as a student tour director, I gathered a group of eighth graders in front of the main entrance of the National World War II Memorial in the nation's capital so that they can get a clear view of the Washington Monument across 17th Street. Tourists love to pose for the requisite photo of the monument between their fingers, making it look as though they are holding it in their hand, like the photos I have seen of the Tower of Pisa. Most students gather together to help each other get that perfectly placed photo. However, this particular day I saw a group of boys lying down on the ground while others aimed their smart phones in their direction. I was confused, so I motioned to one of their teachers.

"What are they doing?"

"Look. Stand here and you can see the picture they are taking."

The middle school boys were giving themselves a giant erection that looked just like the satyrs. In all fairness to the boys, the Egyptian obelisk served both as a form of sun worship as well as a phallic symbol representing fertility and power. Adolescent boys on the verge of puberty suffer from raging hormones. In an uncharacteristic moment of whimsy, I walked up to one of the boys and whispered: "You wish!" From then on, I advised the students that they take photos only in the upright position.

I set eyes on a much different angle of the male genitalia on a trip to Vietnam later that year. Our tour director, Thuyen, recommended that we not miss the architectural garden, a re-creation of different types of ethnic houses at the Vietnam Museum of Ethnology. The structures included wooden tombs that served as the final resting place for whole families. The tomb houses of the Girai people, one of the ethnic minorities in Vietnam, were adorned with wooden figures carved out of tree trunks, each one boasting either a gigantic phallus or a women's genitalia.

Even at our advancing age, many of us giggled, perhaps out of embarrassment in the company of others. Off on my own, I scrutinized one of the wooden couples whose faces reminded me of the monolithic human statues of Easter Island, although I had only seen them in photos and a singular one in a museum. Their faces were indistinguishable, but their sex was clear. The man aimed his oversized phallus at the woman's bare breasts and baby-filled belly. Those eighth-grade boys back in Washington would have been quite envious of the gentleman. Actually, no man could measure up to those wooden penises, but the carvings were not a symbol of a man's prowess, but an embodiment of fertility, of both the family and the harvest. I was being a silly tourist taking delight in the consortium of cocks.

Although Susan traveled with me to Vietnam, she missed the fertility carvings. Not having much interest in history, she decided to forgo a visit to the ethnological museum. She might have joined us had she known about the penises. I don't remember where she might have gone, perhaps in search of her man of the day. Susan is not a dumb blonde. Once flaxen, she now sports a stylish hue of platinum. She is not stupid. She knows numbers, finances, and people. However, she's considerably less enthusiastic about history. Her disinterest dates back to her school days. Her college history professor offered Susan a deal: if her final essay contained at least one historically accurate and cogent point, she would pass the class.

The creative essay question asked her to imagine Nikita Khrushchev, Abraham Lincoln, John F. Kennedy, and Napoleon Bonaparte having a discussion at the dinner table. Susan was to compose an exchange among the men that revealed an understanding of the history of their era. Not having any idea when each of these men lived, she wrote an epicurean conversation.

"So, Mr. Khrushchev, how is your steak?" asked President Kennedy.

Khrushchev answered, "A little overdone, but I do like my Brussel sprouts."

Lincoln, who didn't particularly like vegetables added: "I am not a fan of Brussel sprouts, but I agree with my Russian friend, Khrushchev. The steak is a bit well done."

"I am hoping for a napoleon for dessert. The French really know how to do pastry," Napoleon replied. Needless to say, Susan failed the history class, although her professor had several chuckles.

A good travel partner, nevertheless, Susan acquiesced to join me on a train ride from Sorrento for a visit to Pompeii. She wasn't interested in Pompeii any more than the Hanoi museum, especially since she had already visited on an earlier trip with different friends, but she acquiesced to accompany me on the train to visit the ruins. However, she insisted that I didn't need to hire one of the many guides hawking their services at the entrance to the uncovered city, frozen in time by the merciless eruption of Mt. Vesuvius.

"You have a map. It's just ruins. You can walk around on your own," she insisted. Against my better judgement, I heeded her advice, almost missing the penises of Pompeii altogether.

We decided to split up. I wanted to explore and photograph the remains of the denizens of the once vibrant city, many frozen in action, and she wanted to give it a quick glimpse before finding a place to sit and read. The plan was to meet up in a couple of hours. After leaving Susan at the entrance, I made a circuitous route around the ruins, back-tracking, and nearly tripping over cracked stones. I hoped to locate the notorious brothels of Pompeii, especially the Lupanar, or whore house, to witness the erotic wall paintings. According to the map, phalluses were engraved in the street or carved into the stone on the facades of the buildings to point the way. While I was circling the ruins looking for phallic signs, Susan was content sitting and reading, until she wasn't.

I had no idea where I was. I was frustrated, hot, and hungry. Instead of a brothel filled with erotic sculptures, I discovered a cafeteria where I took care of both my stomach and my bladder. Refreshed, I continued on my quest and was thrilled to see the first sign of a phallus on the front of a crumbling portico. Suddenly, I realized that the street was peppered with penises, all leading me to the Grand Brothel of Pompeii. These were elegantly carved inside what appeared to be a small temple housing a gigantic penis. Others, especially on the stone streets, were simple phalluses carved out of a boulder. Unfortunately, I wasted so much time in search of the phalluses I only had a few minutes to explore the erotica.

On my way out, I stepped into one of the private residences, the House of Faun. One particular room had a mosaic of a satyr and a nymph in a type of foreplay. The man had the pointy ears of a goat but the muscular legs of a man, and the woman was full-figured and tiled in a lighter shade than the gentleman, more romantic than erotic. The nymph gently laid her head on his shoulder while he held one of her arms to his chest. I wanted one just like it for my living room.

Sadly, I had overstayed my brief visit to Pompeii, and I had to curtail my penile curiosity, returning to my travel partner waiting for me back at the entrance. By the time I met Susan, she was anxious to return to our home base in Sorrento.

"I almost left without you!" she announced. But she didn't, and both feeling a bit disappointed, we headed back to the train station.

I discovered more ancient erotica on my trip to India on a visit to Khajuraho, a UNESCO World Heritage site of twenty-five ornate Hindu and Jain temples built over a span of one hundred years a millennium after the destruction of Pompeii. The center of the Chandela Dynasty, Khajuraho fell to Muslim invaders who destroyed and desecrated many of the temples. Other structures were lost to time until a British engineer, T.S. Burt, rediscovered the glorious temples in 1838.

Our local tour director, Dil, led us through the maze of edifices, pointing out the intricate decorations both inside and out. Eventually, she led us to the erotic carvings, stopping in front of a bas-relief of an elephant with his head and chest adorned with jewels. "This is Ganesha, one of the most worshipped gods in Hinduism. What do you notice about him?"

I noticed that his trunk was entwined between his tusk and his leg. Next to him stood a man making love to an extremely supple woman. She had her head bent back, almost touching the floor, one hand on the ground for balance and the other on the knee of her lover. I thought she was quite nimble, but I didn't contribute to the discussion.

Another guest answered, "He's watching them having sex." The man had an astonishing way with words.

I think she was testing us to see if we remembered the description of the Hindu god that she had shared earlier in our journey. We had seen many images of Ganesha in our two weeks in India. "Does anyone recall why Ganesha is so revered?"

I waited to see if anyone else answered and, when there was silence, I responded: "I think he is the god of wisdom." I still know how to brown-nose my teacher.

Another person added that she thought he was also the god of luck.

I pondered the sexual image: the god of wisdom and luck looking into the face of a beautiful woman in the throes of an orgasm while she bends over like a performer in Cirque du Soleil. In a very intimate gesture, the gentleman in the bas-relief presses a finger down on her belly. I thought the man and the woman were having a fantastically erotic experience.

Dil interrupted my ruminations with an explanation that coincided with my thoughts: "Flexibility is a virtue. So is the act of sexual intercourse. Life is meant to be enjoyed. *Kuma sutra* is not about sexual positions but about love and the joy it brings to living."

She moved on to another scene on the bas-relief in which the man is lifting a woman on to him while another man helps them balance. A second woman on the other side of the couple masturbates. Just a little further down I found a threesome: the gentleman was enjoying the two women while they satisfied each other. At this point my intellectualism dissipated and penis envy ensued for the first time in a long while. It looked like they were having a great deal more fun than I was.

Erotic as the carvings were, it was difficult to get a good view of a penis since it was usually doing its business inside a woman's vagina or mouth, or, in one case, a horse. One of the most famous bas-reliefs includes a man forcing his very large phallus into a mare who is oblivious to his actions. Although another man standing behind the horse closes his eyes, perhaps condemning such practice that goes against Hindu doctrine, the man in front of the horse is satisfying himself.

The erotic carvings are limited to the outside façade of the temple, where worldly pleasures exist. As our guide explained, Hinduism regards sexual pleasure an essential and divine part of life. Inside was devoid of earthly pleasures, instead focusing on the spiritual. Dil offered us different theories behind the sensual art: It could have served as delight and amusement for the royalty who indulged in luxurious living or perhaps it was used to educate the young men in *Kama Sutra*, the art of living well. *Kama*, translated to "pleasure" in English, is one of the four permissible goals of Hindu life, the others being righteousness (*Dharma*), prosperity (*Artha*), and liberation (*Moksha*). My interest in the erotic carvings didn't entirely distract me from Dil's religious commentary.

Cultures around the world grant magical powers to the phallus. It was a source of luck to the agrarian Sicilians, which might explain the phallic symbols my girlfriends and I discovered on a tour of the Italian island. Susan and I planned a private tour with a Sicilian destination management company for a week's adventure. Since the price of the tour would go down significantly with a full car, we invited six other women to join us. Regrettably, Susan's bad back caused her to pull out shortly before the trip, and I found myself in Italy with six other wonderful women whom I didn't know very well.

Our journey began in the city of Taormina, perched high on a hilltop on the east coast of the island. As we walked the steep, narrow stone steps, we were struck by the omnipresent pairs of ceramic Moorish heads, or *Teste di Moro*, depicting a fair-skinned woman and a man with North

African features. The colorful heads were everywhere, many with plants blooming from the center. Later, when we met our adorably handsome Sicilian guide, Rosario, he told us the story of the original legend.

"There once was a Moorish merchant who, upon visiting Palermo, fell in love with a beautiful Sicilian girl with whom he had a passionate love affair. Upon learning that her lover had a wife and children back home, she became enraged, and, in a fit of anger, she cut off her lover's head. Wanting to keep him close to her, she turned his severed head into a pot in which she grew an amazingly fertile basil plant. The people of Palermo thought the basil was so lovely that they recreated the pot in ceramics, hoping their own such plant would similarly blossom."

"But what about the penises?" asked one of my fellow travelers.

"What penises?"

"We saw some of those pots with colorful phalluses on top."

Rosario answered, "I'm not sure what you are talking about."

"Really," thought more than one of us. "How did he miss the penises?"

"You will have to show me."

Before leaving the site of traditional ceramics, Rosario offered us a little more background. "The iconic ceramic heads are adorned with Baroque details and glazed in the Maiolica style, a refined, white-glazed pottery popular during the Italian Renaissance. Now they can be found all over Sicily, on balconies, in gardens, and as wall decorations."

We had seen the pots with the suggestive penises in jewelry stores that adorned the steep stone streets. Spotted yellow phalluses of varied sizes emerged out of the Moor's crown, each topped with a red, blue, or green head. Jewelry hung from each of the colorful shafts. Additional penises hung down from the bottom of his hat, whimsically painted with flowers and other designs. Browsing necklaces dangling from penises was a bit bizarre. As we continued to walk along the narrow streets of Taormina, often so steep that steps brought us up and down, we finally spotted one of the iconic heads with colorful phalluses adorning his crown.

"Those? I think they are just playful attempts to get your attention. They don't have anything to do with Sicilian history or culture."

I wasn't satisfied with Rosario's answer, so I googled it. Without any specific reference to the use of phallic symbols in the jewelry shops of Taormina, I was required to use my sharp skills of deductive reasoning.

Sicily, of course, was a part of the ancient Roman Empire that considered phalluses as a symbol of power and strength. The penis summoned the powers of Fascinus, the god of power, depicted as a winged phallus with a penis for a tail and penises for legs. Ancient Romans wore pendants and other jewelry depicting Fascinus the same way I might wear a Hamsa, an open hand with an eye embedded in the open palm. Rosario was probably correct in his assessment of the phalluses as an enticement to enter the store, but I like to think the shopkeepers were offering a nod to their Roman culture.

After witnessing our excitement over our phallic discovery, I am surprised that Rosario didn't mention the most extravagant array of phalluses in Sicily – the penis café, Bar Turrisi, high atop the city in Castelmola. There we could have handled numerous phalluses, from the front door handle to the faucet in the bathroom. The café, which had been owned by generations of the Turrisi family since 1947, is not meant to be vulgar, but to celebrate life, very much like the sacred temples of Khajuraho. Next time.

A discussion of penises on tour cannot conclude without recounting the sighting of the largest one I have ever seen. It didn't belong to a god or a human statue. It was dangling from an elephant. On our safari in Chobe National Park in Botswana, home of over 120,000 elephants, my daughter and I were feasting our eyes on the remarkable expanse of pachyderms when we heard a passenger in our jeep ask, "Does that elephant have five legs?"

Everyone turned in the direction he was pointing to glimpse an elephant on the other side of the Chobe River. The bull looked as though he had three back legs, with one resting just inches above the grass. Snickering, our safari guide answered our stares: "That, ladies and gentlemen, is not his leg. It is his penis." I thought it actually looked like a second trunk between his hind limbs, rather than a fifth leg.

"The elephant's penis is prehensile. That means, like his trunk, it can grasp things. He can even use it to hold himself up," our driver guide added. I wondered how many of the men were wondering if that was a trick they would like to perform, although it would also be quite difficult to hide the member in their pants. Then, to our amazement, the elephant used his penis to swat insects from his underside.

"Weighing around six tons, the bull needs the massive penis to help him maneuver during mating. He can use it to locate the opening of the cow, thrusting with all of its strength. The shaft does all of the work so that the elephant doesn't have to use his muscles." It might be nice to avoid the salty sweat and wet shine of sexual intercourse. Our driver continued our safari, and I put the humongous penis out of my mind until my daughter gifted me a photo book with the picture of the phallus, so, like an elephant, I'll never forget.

6

WOMEN

Amazing how eye and skin color come in many shades yet many think sexuality is just gay or straight.

DaShane Stokes

I unexpectedly found myself discussing my love life with my rabbi one morning, soon after he performed my Jewish divorce ceremony. Paul and I were already divorced and neither of us had felt the need to obtain Jewish divorce papers, or a *gett*. That was until he and his fiancé were planning their wedding and their rabbi refused to marry them without one.

My memory of the *gett* is clouded with humiliation. I have a flashback of a piece of paper being thrown at me and having to walk backwards, away from Paul. Years later, Rabbi Aft corrected my memory. Since we had already been divorced in a civil court, there was no need for mediation by the *Beit Din*, or Jewish court. Rabbi Aft represented us in front of the *Beit Din*, obtaining permission to perform the religious ceremony divorcing us in the eyes of Jewish law. First, the rabbi asked me to remove any jewelry from my hands. My wedding and engagement rings were long gone. After assuring that no one, including our witness, wished to protest the divorce proceeding, the rabbi directed me to hold my hands together with open palms. He instructed Paul to drop the small packet that held the *gett* into my cupped hands.

The rabbi then asked Paul to repeat after him: "This is your *gett* and with it you are divorced from this time forth so that you are free of the past and free to live your life in the future as you see fit." Paul repeated after him, having to pause once for a reminder of the long, convoluted sentence.

I received the document and walked the short distance back to the rabbi who proceeded to cut the four corners of the *gett* so that the document could not be reused by others, as though anyone would actually recycle a divorce paper! Despite the years of living my life the way I wanted, a Jewish court had just given me permission to do so. And Paul had permission to remarry.

Soon after my Jewish divorce, I set up a meeting with Rabbi Aft to discuss my lapsed Judaism since separating from both Paul and the Jewish camp that had been my second home for thirteen years. My rabbi was also "Bruce" to me, a member of our camp board of directors and a colleague. I didn't feel comfortable at synagogue anymore, especially since the first time I ran into Paul and his wife at services. Rabbi Aft was empathetic to my concerns. When he suggested I might join a different temple with a more active single population, the discussion morphed into the topic of dating. I answered with a litany of complaints about the lack of desirable single men.

"Have you ever considered dating a woman? As you probably know, a couple of our female congregants have turned to women for intimate companionship."

I was stunned. I lied to my rabbi: "No. Not really."

Although he embodied broadmindedness in many religious manners, he still held on to a few conservative beliefs. For instance, he refused to perform the wedding ceremony for my son's interfaith marriage. Now his free thinking surprised me. Of course, I had considered it. I had had a couple of relationships with women, but gender blindness was not an issue I was ready to discuss with him.

My first female crush was in college, after I began dating Paul. One of the better attributes of our relationship was that we were honest with each other. Not only was Paul open to my fondness of women, but he also encouraged it. Some men like that sort of thing. After all, when we started dating in 1972, we were in the midst of the sexual revolution. The object of my affection was a petite powerhouse of talent, but when I revealed my feelings, she explained that she was flattered, but she was not interested.

My first relationship after my separation from Paul was with a woman. I had a bad taste in my mouth for men. I foolishly thought that a woman wouldn't be as controlling. Jo was a petite, first-generation Chinese American who rose to success in the public sector of finance. She almost always wore dark three-piece pantsuits with a starched white button-down shirt. Her raven-black hair was cut in a short pixie. She flowered me with gifts and devotion. After the tragic events of September 11, we became each other's moral support, spending hours watching the terror replayed on television. Later in the month, we were watching the telethon, "America: A Tribute to Heroes," when Jo offered an invitation no travel addict would refuse: "Please come to San Francisco with me."

In a bizarre twist, no one knew about Jo except for Paul, and it was my little secret that I didn't want to share with the world. I wasn't very open-minded about my own affections. I liked her, and she liked me, and we both happened to be female. My inability to feel comfortable with a woman outside of our private space made traveling with Jo difficult. If she tried to show any sign of affection in public, I brushed her away. As we walked through Chinatown, Jo attempted to take my hand, which I quickly drew back. She returned my rebuke with a wounded look before buying me an exquisitely embroidered Chinese robe, as if to say, "Look what I can give you."

The power struggle continued throughout the trip. Jo caressed my shoulder as she pulled out a chair for me in a restaurant, and I recoiled. She took me to the now-defunct Tommy Toy's Cuisine Chinois where the likes of Francis Ford Coppola and Dianne Feinstein dined in an opulent setting reminiscent of an Imperial Chinese palace. We enjoyed their six-course signature dinner of crispy prawns with an amazing blend of Chinese spices, a seafood bisque cooked in a coconut and topped with puff pastry, a whole lobster as our third course, followed by Peking Duck. The fifth course was a combination of medallions of filet mignon served with asparagus and rice. Dessert was a peach mousse in strawberry coulis. She wooed me with food. I might have let her hold my hand on the way back to the hotel.

The following day Jo bought us tickets for the Wine Train, a journey through the Napa Valley with more food and, of course, wine. We sat behind a narrow table perpendicular to the train's window, allowing us to observe the spectacular vineyards and scenery while dining on a four-course lunch. After sipping wine with lunch, we drank several more glasses at two local vineyards. I was relaxed and very happy and a little drunk.

I have never joined the mile-high club, but that day I came close to joining the slow-moving train club. I retired to the bathroom when I heard a knock on the door. I explained that the toilet was occupied, but the voice on the other side said she knew and instructed me to open the door. I wasn't comfortable kissing Jo in public, but in the bathroom the drink and romance usurped my apprehension. When the two of us finally stepped out of the small lavatory, the little girl waiting outside the door looked very confused.

The romance of travel moderated my anxiety about having a relationship with a woman, but our contrasting comfort levels with each other often caused us to clash. Jo was proud to be a dyke, and I was a bi-curious woman with severe collywobbles about the relationship. After our California expedition, I explained to Jo that I couldn't connect with her in a way that she wanted. In fact, she was smothering me. Yet, she continued to send gifts. First there was a duvet set that I had admired in Bloomingdales that I thought was too expensive. That was followed by a VCR player. She knew mine had died. I tried to return them to no avail. When the gold necklace arrived, it was time to be resolute: "I am not your girlfriend, and there is no relationship. You have to stop sending gifts." Jo finally heard me. I was single once again.

Jo hadn't worked out very well, but our time together taught me that I still enjoyed a private, intimate relationship with a woman. I decided I was a plesbian or part-time lesbian, according to the online *Urban Dictionary*. I needed to find a woman more like me, but that was not a thought I wanted to share with Rabbi Aft. Then, I found her. She was married with children still at home. She was safe because, like me, Mindy was bi-curious, a like-minded plesbian.

We developed a sporadic relationship since she was still caring for her young teens and trying to work things out with her bipolar husband. But we could travel together. If Mindy had chosen to go on vacation with a man, it would have been an obvious breach of the marriage. Women, however, travel together all the time. Making travel arrangements for a conference in Montreal, I discovered it is was much cheaper to fly into Burlington, Vermont, and drive to Canada. We decided it was the perfect opportunity to spend a long weekend together in the Green Mountain State before I joined a colleague for the ride to Montreal.

I found a quaint bed and breakfast on the website for the Vermont Gay Tourism Association, a modern-day version of the *Green Book,* only for the LBGT community to find gay-friendly and gay-accommodating lodgings. The violet window shutters and front door of the Phineas Swann were balanced by a pale lilac exterior. We stayed in the main house in the "Green Room" with its four-poster bed and Victorian furnishings. It was a little piece of paradise, and it was ours for three days.

With two teenage girls and a despondent spouse at home, Mindy relished her liberty on our brief sojourn. We were staying in the small town of Montgomery Center, northeast of Burlington, about twenty miles from the Canadian border. Both of us wanted to explore the area, and, for the most part, we were two good friends on a lovely mountain vacation.

Although Vermont is not known for good wine, we discovered a family-owned winery in Cambridge, about halfway between Burlington and Stowe. We enjoyed a glass of unexceptional wine on their patio, overlooking the verdant mountains and wild flower gardens. Sitting there with her was unlike anything I felt when I was with Jo. This was safe.

The B&B served a lovely afternoon tea. As Mindy and I were enjoying our tea and biscuits in the sitting room of the Phineas Swann, we came upon a brochure about the covered bridges of Montgomery. According to the pamphlet, wooden bridges were covered as a protection against the harsh Vermont climate and were used as a type of message board announcing local events, "...and most always, to meet a beloved sweetheart." Romantic bridges aren't limited to Madison County. We decided to follow the map to locate the seven covered bridges, all built by the same brothers, Sheldon and Savannah Jewitt.

The first bridge Mindy and I encountered was a red ramshackle lattice structure with a floor too damaged to cross, rendering it dangerous as a "kissing bridge." The next bridge, the white-washed Longley, crossed the Trout River, allowing for charming landscape photos. The Hopkins Bridge also appeared safe for a walk through. Visitors had left their names and initials carved in the interior lattice wood. I thought we might see more signs of amorous couples, but "Sandra and Dan" were outweighed by a lot of individual initials and dates scratched into bridge as if to say, "I was here." We didn't leave any such markings, nor did we share a romantic kiss. We were tourists more than lovers.

The next day was the Fourth of July, and the small town of Enosburg Falls found the perfect spot for their fireworks in front of the local mortuary. A banner attached to the entrance of Spears Funeral Home also announced that it was the location of the Strawberry Festival. You could enjoy eating fresh strawberries and watching fireworks before burying your beloved. Mindy and I sat next to each other, enjoying the company and the pretty awesome fireworks for a tiny town. Displays of affection were left to the privacy of our room.

The rest of the trip was filled with typical tourist ventures, including Ben and Jerry's, the Shelburne Museum, and the quaint ski town of Stowe. It was easy to be with Mindy: she laughed at my silly stories and listened more than she talked, complementing my incessant chatter. We enjoyed our meals together with no judgment. She had no desire for control in our relationship. And so, two years later, when I opened one of my travel deal emails to discover a five-day trip to Madrid for less than $500, including airfare, she was the perfect companion.

The departure was reminiscent of my trip to Morocco with Rachel. A light snow started the night before we were supposed to leave. My sleep was interrupted repeatedly throughout the night by the sound of ice striking my bedroom windows. My alarm radio woke me to the news that not only were schools closed, but all the offices, including mine, were shut as well. It's rare to close the county's school administration offices, so the roads must have been treacherous.

When I called the airline, I was treated to an interminable time listening to on-hold music. When an agent finally answered, I asked about flight delays and cancellations.

The agent was not optimistic. "We are confident that this storm is going to have a significant impact on flights. Your flight from D.C. to Philly might be able to take off, but I would be very surprised if there will be any flights out of Philadelphia this evening."

When I followed up with a call to the tour operator, their agent was taken aback by the airline's assessment of the situation. She explained that their offices sat outside of Philadelphia, and most of the flights were departing, although not necessarily on time. We continued checking the flights throughout the day – Mindy from home in Maryland and me from Virginia. I lived inside the Capital Beltway. She lived far north of the interstate highway that encircles Washington, D.C. We tried to be positive and each of us made a reservation with a shared van service.

I was in the van on my way to the airport when Mindy called to tell me that SuperShuttle had no drivers to transport her to the airport. The phone call with that information came just at the reserved time of the pickup. Her husband was at work and taxis were backed up, so Mindy had no other option than to drive herself.

I am glad that, like me, she performed the ritual of checking her passport one more time after filling her tank with gas. Mindy had inadvertently picked up the one that had expired. After circling home for the correct passport, we met up at the airport with two hours to spare.

Madrid, like Vermont, was four days of blissful exploration and affection without the pressure to be anything more. We dined al fresco in the warmth of the 60-degree February sun, leaving the ice and snow well behind us. Mindy and I strolled the plazas, admiring the exquisite facades of the buildings. We might have held hands.

As a Catholic, Mindy very much wanted to visit the Royal Basilica of San Francisco el Grande. Unfortunately, the tour was in Spanish, and neither of us were able to understand the guide, but we wondered at the neoclassical architecture of the monumental church. Even more remarkable were the works of art that adorned the basilica, including Zubarán's paintings of St. Francis of Assisi, the patron saint of animals and the environment, and Goya's *The Sermon of Saint Bernardino of Siena*, in which the artist paints himself into the crowd. We were oblivious of the irony of two plesbians, including one Jewess, admiring the painting. Two of St. Bernardine's most popular subjects were sodomy and Judaism. According to Daniel Horan, a Franciscan monk, St. Bernadino's sermons were riddled with ostensible anti-Semitism and homophobia, although the learned monk attributes that to the time and culture of 15th century. We simply appreciated the splendor of the art. There was a silence between us until, at the same time, we said we were ready to go.

Mindy and I walked the long distance from our hotel to the Plaza España and the Cervantes Memorial. I had never read Cervantes' *Don Quixote*, but I had seen performances of *Man of La Mancha*, including the original Broadway show with Richard Kiley and Joan Diener. My first girl crush played Aldonza, Don Quixote's love interest, in our college production of the musical. I could mouth most of the words of the songs. I wanted to see the iconic statue of Don Quixote on his horse and Sancho on his donkey.

One of the largest squares in Madrid, Plaza España is surrounded by skyscrapers, restaurants, and shops. In the middle of the plaza stands Miguel de Cervantes, overlooking his two famous creations – Don Quixote and Sancho. The two bronze men looked as though they were ready to ride into the pool in front of them. As Mindy and I walked around to examine them more closely, I started singing "To dream the impossible dream, to fight the unbeatable foe, to bear with unbearable sorrow, to run where the brave dear not go." Rather than walk away in embarrassment, my girlfriend laughed with joy. Mindy is one of my only friends or family who thinks I am funny.

The night before our flight home, I checked our paper itinerary, but, rather than looking at the departure time from Madrid, my eyes went to the arrival time in Philadelphia. The next morning, we were showering and taking our leisure time to dress. Mindy was putting on her make-up when my anxiety compelled me to check our flight information again.

"SHIT! Our flight is at 12:40, not 3:40!"

It was nine in the morning, and I was in a state of panic. On our arrival to Madrid, the taxi ride from the airport to the hotel had taken us almost an hour, and we were supposed to check in at the airport three hours before the flight. The only time on our trip that we had words was when Mindy continued putting on her mascara while I ran around the hotel room like a buffoon.

"Forget the make-up. You can finish on the way to the airport. I'm going to run down to the front desk and ask them to call us a taxi. Grab everything. We have to go!"

I can perform miracles in a state of anxiety, and, within ten minutes, we were sitting in a taxi on the way to Madrid-Barajas Airport. I tried to breathe slowly while she took out a compact mirror and finished her face. The first taxi driver must have taken us for a ride since this time we were at the airport in thirty minutes for half the cost, even with hitting traffic along the route. Luckily, the lines at check in, as well as security, were short, and we even had time for last-minute souvenir shopping.

We never broke up. Instead, our relationship evolved into a close friendship, and then, as our lives became busy with other friends and family, we drifted apart. She moved north, and I moved south.

Gender blindness assumes a physical attraction to an individual, rather than to a man or a woman. My rabbi understood that. My friends in the know suggest that all I have to do is to meet the right person, whether male or female. My other friends say that all I have to do is meet the right man. These days, I am not in the mood for either.

7

LOST

Your grandma always had a terrible sense of direction. She could get lost on an escalator.

Fredrik Backman, *And Every Morning the Way Home*

I drove in the wrong direction on a one-way street on my first road test. I remember the examiner screaming something like "Where the hell are you going?" It was no surprise when I received my failure notice from the New York DMV. My father once told me I couldn't find my way out of a paper bag.

Since I have no sense of direction, it is logical that I am afraid of getting lost, and, when I get lost, I panic. My pulse races. I make more wrong turns. I become disoriented and then paralyzed. Tears ensue, and it usually takes someone else to get me out of my predicament, like a phone call to my dad or my son, both of whom have a remarkable sense of wayfinding. Eventually, my fear of getting lost was minimized by the incredible invention of the Global Positioning System, but I didn't get my first Garmin GPS until age 48, so there were a lot of tears and collywobbles until past middle age.

I was 43 when I picked up my son on his first return home from college for Thanksgiving. His train to Union Station was arriving late in the evening, past Paul's bedtime. I drove to D.C. from the Virginia suburbs, but found myself in a nearby high-crime neighborhood instead of the train station. I was adrift in a maze of streets that do not lie parallel, but, instead, cross at angles, coming together at confusing intersections. It was dark and I was lost.

I was still dating Jo at the time, so I called her because she had an incredible sense of direction. She worked near the National Mall and knew the District well. As she attempted to figure out where I was in order to direct me to the train station, I frantically made a left turn without checking for approaching vehicles, unthinkingly cutting off a police car. The sound of his siren was immediate. After I pulled off to the side, he approached my car, and I turned into a bowl of mush.

"I am so sorry. I am so sorry. I am so lost, and my son is coming home from college, and I can't find the station, and he doesn't have a phone, and he is not going to know where I am and my friend was just trying to help me get there and I didn't see you coming and I am so sorry. I am so scared." Tears and shallow breaths were coming in between each word.

"Ma'am take a breath." It turns out that I had almost plowed into a sympathetic cop.

"Where are you trying to go?"

"Union Station."

I was expecting a lecture about driving and talking on the phone, but, instead, he offered to escort me to the train station.

"Follow me. I'll take you to the train."

I waved my unlimited gratitude as I saw my son exiting the front doors to meet me.

Wayfinding isn't, in point of fact, a sense at all since it involves our use of multiple intellects such as our ability to understand where we are in relationship to our surroundings and our awareness of spatial orientation and balance. My spatial intelligence scores on standardized tests in school were mediocre at best. I have trouble determining direction despite having walked or driven in the area for years.

Sometimes my method of defeating my directionally challenged brain takes an unusual turn, dangerously bordering on stereotyping. One of my early post-Paul trips was a whirlwind journey through Scandinavia and Russia. After a morning tour of our arrival city, Copenhagen, I wanted to visit the Danish Jewish Museum. We had not yet had an opportunity to socialize with our fellow travelers, so I was still very much on my own. After leaving the group at the National Museum, I opened my tourist map of the city in an attempt to locate my destination. According to the map, the museum was on a small island separated by the NyHaven, or

"New Harbor," and three small tributaries. I had enough wayfinding ability to know that I needed to cross water, but I was confused about which direction to walk.

I looked up from the map to see an older couple from my tour group. My instinct told me that they were most likely going to the Jewish Museum. I may not have a sense of direction, but if there is any validity to the belief that Jews have a sensing device to detect other Jews, or Jewdar, it worked for me that day. Such beliefs can be construed as anti-Semitic, but, in this case, I rightfully assumed they were headed to the same place, and, after introductions, they allowed me to tag along with them.

As I walked into the museum space, I felt disoriented, even a bit wobbly. The architect, Daniel Libeskind, angled the walls and the floor so that my movement through the exhibit felt unsteady, like Jewish immigrants to Denmark making their way through their new country. Or, as the museum literature suggests, the precarious trip Jewish Danes made in October 1943, escaping the Nazis to neutral Sweden with the help of their Christian brethren. If Libeskind wanted me to feel seasick and uneasy like those Jews on their escape, he triumphed in his design. Early in our visit, Carol, the female half of the Jewish couple, and I joined elbows, steadying each other as we walked between the artifacts.

Without reading an explanation in the museum's brochure, I would not have recognized that the path we were walking, with what I thought were sharp haphazard turns, was actually spelling out the Hebrew word, *mitzvah*, the word that also crafts the museum's logo. A *mitzvah*, simply put, is a good deed: the Danes wrought a great deed, saving over ninety percent of their Jewish citizens.

As we exited the building, Carol, Bernie, and I stopped to introduce ourselves formally. Bernie, with a head full of white hair, stood only an inch taller than Carol, looking at least ten years younger than he, with her perfectly coiffed blonde hair and round face sans wrinkles. Although we were already in the digital age, Carol carried a throw-away camera to capture her holiday. I asked the requisite questions one asks fellow travelers on a tour: "Where are you from?"

"Florida, in the Boca Raton area. You?"

"D.C." I never answer "Virginia" – it's too far South. "I live in Old Town Alexandria." It was time to play Jewish geography.

"Really? Carol's daughter lives in Old Town—on Prince Street." That brief sentence held two important facts: this was their second marriage, or, at least hers, and that Carol's daughter lived less than two blocks from my place. Carol and Bernie would become my friends. Sometimes it pays to get lost.

A number of tour directing colleagues believed I had no business being in the guiding business. There is validity that a lack of wayfinding is a hindrance to a guide. On my first and only large choir trip as the tour escort in New York, I became lost between the baggage claim and bus pick-up at LaGuardia Airport. I knew Dulles and National well, but the New York airports create tremendous angst because of their size and labyrinthine configuration. I became totally *farblunget*, or hopelessly lost and unsure of where to turn next, trying to escort forty students, many of their parents, and their wheelchair-bound choir director from arrivals in a terminal at LaGuardia to our two chartered motor coaches. There are mindsets that are best described in Yiddish.

I had never met a student tour at the New York airport, and I foolishly didn't scope it out before the group arrived. But I knew the procedure at the D.C. airports and assumed it was the same: I wait for the group to exit the gate area, usually after they take half an hour to go to the bathroom, escort them to baggage claim to get their luggage, and call the driver as the last suitcase is claimed. He then pulls up to the front of the terminal where the group boards the motor coach. This driver had a different idea.

"Hello, Joe. This is Faye, your tour escort. We have all of our luggage and we are ready to be picked up."

"You have to come to me." My nerves started to prickle.

"What do you mean? Where are you?"

"In the motor coach parking lot."

"Where is that?"

"Outside the terminal."

"Do you know how I get to you?" That was not as stupid a question as it seems since there were three levels to enter and exit.

"I don't know. It's where we always pick up."

"Well, this is my first time I'm meeting a group here, and I have a teacher in a wheelchair. I need you to come to us."

"I can't do that." I made my next mistake at that moment. Of course, he could do it. He just didn't want to, and I was too diffident to argue with him.

I had a trainee on tour with me, so I pulled Andy to the side to explain the situation and asked him to bring up the rear. Since the teacher's husband, who was four decades older than Andy, was getting winded wheeling his wife, Andy grabbed the chair. Andy was from Seattle, and he had never been to LaGuardia either. I was supposed to be teaching him the ropes, and I wasn't exactly doing a good job.

The recently renovated Terminal C had four levels at the time, and I had no idea where to go. I proceeded to ask an airport employee for the location of the buses.

"I think it's on the first level. You can go out those stairs over there."

That was the moment of my next error. Notice that he said, "I think," and he did so without conviction.

We played follow-the-leader with over forty students and twenty parents, all with suitcases in hand, with Andy and Mrs. Kingman as the wheelchair-bound caboose. They deviated from us to look for an elevator to the first floor while the rest of us went down two flights of concrete to find no sign of any motor coaches. We went back into the building, meeting the wheelchair as it came out of the elevator.

"I am so sorry, but someone gave me the wrong directions." I knew that was a lame excuse. I stopped someone else who appeared to be a little more assured and, once again, asked for directions to the bus lot.

"You need to go to the third floor. Follow the signs to parking."

I wasn't sure how to find any other stairs, so we went back outside while the wheelchair, with its very unhappy occupant, waited for the elevator to return to where we began this mess.

When we reconvened on the third floor, I located the sign for parking and, with everyone in tow, we walked into a garage full of cars. The familiar signs of anxiety were rushing over me and, when they did, I continued to make bad choices. While Andy stayed with the group, I ran around like the proverbial chicken without a head until I saw a uniformed guide who, I hoped, knew more than the last two people I trusted.

I whispered, afraid my group might hear me. "Please, I am so lost. I have a large group, and we are looking for our bus."

"The motor coach lot is on the middle level. You can actually go right outside on the second floor. You can't miss it."

We had walked down from the third floor to the first floor and back up, and we most certainly did miss it.

The students were getting hungry and tired, the parents were becoming frustrated, and the choir leader was fuming. We had a Broadway show that evening, and everyone needed to have lunch and dress for the theater. Mrs. Kingman had not yet said anything to me, but the look of disdain spoke for itself. After descending another flight of stairs, we finally found our two buses ready to load, over an hour after the group had landed. Needless to say, the choir leader and I didn't quite hit it off. She told my boss that I was "the tour escort from hell." I deserved it, well, maybe just a little bit.

But like most people with a learning disability, I have learned to compensate. For example, I use landmarks to know where to turn. If I can, I walk the route before meeting the group, noting markers along the way. If I don't have time to do that, I figure out the directions using a map app, noting the names of shops and restaurants as indicators. After being dubbed the "tour escort from hell," I don't trust myself to locate a pick-up spot. I ask for help. There are numerous Facebook pages for tour directors with very willing experts to tell me where to go. My ultimate goal is to look like I know where I am going and to do it with finesse.

Touring Manhattan by foot or bus is easy since the city is designed on a grid. All one needs to know is if you are going uptown, downtown, or cross town. Avenues go up and down, and numbered streets go cross town. It helps to know that twenty streets add up to a mile when your guests ask if they can walk from the Empire State Building to Central Park, 34th to 59th Street. If you don't want to get confused or lost, it's also important to know the dividing point for east and west is Fifth Avenue. I have walked in the wrong direction – several times.

The distance between avenues is almost twice as long as the streets. The avenues, unlike the streets, are not all numbered. You need to know that between Third Avenue is Lexington, Park, and Madison and then Fifth Avenue. You can find a few blocks of Fourth Avenue between Bowery and 14th Streets, but the rest of it was renamed Park Street for the beautiful greenway in the middle of the road. Lower Manhattan, the oldest part of the city, is off the grid, with street names like Pearl, Canal, and Delancey, creating an urban maze. Leading a group through downtown — the financial district, Chinatown, and Little Italy — made me very nervous. I appreciated tour operators who hired city guides where I can take up the rear, as long as they don't cause me to miss a step on the sidewalk.

Student groups often use the subway for transit since it is more reliable and often faster than a motor coach. It also offers a definitive New York experience. In her book *Lox, Stocks, and Broadway: The Iconic Trades of New York City,* Nancy Groce describes its mass transit as "New York City's sixth borough." With 244 miles of routes, the subway creates an underground obstacle for a person like me, never sure where to enter or exit, always afraid of riding the rails to eternity.

But there is another technological tool, a directionally challenged person's marvel, that not only tells me which station to use and which train to take, but also tells me how many steps to walk and how many stations we pass before our stop. I am indebted to Nigerian entrepreneur Chinedu Echerou, who, in 2005, created an amazing app called Hop-Stop. Ten years later he sold it to Apple for around one billion dollars; they subsequently discontinued its use. I need not worry about getting lost on the subway, however, since Citymapper has replaced it to tell me the best route available.

The first time I rode the subway with a tour group was on a visit to the World Trade Center site, still an unfinished memorial, followed by lunch in Chinatown. My goal was to take the correct exit from the underground station, find a landmark to know which direction to walk, and then figure out how to get to the sites on our itinerary. And to do all of that not using my phone. I don't generate a chaperone's confidence in me if I am looking down at my cell phone while walking.

After mapping out the subway ride on HopStop, I set out to our first stop at St. Paul's Chapel at Trinity Church Wall Street. I hit the first snag when I lost cellular service underground, unable to use the app to choose the right exit once I arrived at the Fulton Street Station on the number 4 train. If I didn't take the correct exit I would end up walking in circles. I chose an exit at random. As I climbed the garbage-strewn stairs, my phone picked up the network, only to indicate that I was on the wrong side of the street. Rather than crossing above ground, I went back into the subway to find the right exit in order to avoid the same mistake when I was with the group.

Fulton Street and Nassau Street SE Corner. I wrote it down. I climbed back out of the underground and looked up for a sign, a literal sign, not one from a supernatural force. Joe's Pizza was a perfect landmark. Rather than knowing whether to turn right or left, all I needed to do was head toward the ubiquitous Manhattan pizza parlor. Then, I walked past Dunkin Donuts until I saw Broadway with the iconic chapel to the right. I found Trinity Church without getting lost on our tour, although I hid my iPhone with an open Google Maps in my pocket the rest of the day.

If I get lost in my own backyard, imagine my anxiety walking in the maze of the Moroccan medina. On our first day in the Imperial City of Fés, my daughter, Rachel, and I were visiting Fés el-Bali with our small group, where we could shop for souvenirs, including handmade pottery, leather, jewelry, carpets, spices, fruit, and meats. Before our guide, Hassan, walked us into the medina, he introduced us to his helper, a young local lad whose job it was to bring up the rear, making sure not to lose any of us in the souk.

"There are no street signs in the souk, and many stalls look the same. Please keep together, but if you do get separated from us, stay right where you are. We know the medina well, and we will come back to find you," Hassan said.

The medina's labyrinthine paths were claustrophobic, crowded with locals and tourists and flanked by high walls on every side. The aromas of sweet-scented spices and the acrid stench of the leather dyes overwhelmed me. Children helped their parents or grandparents in their stalls while others played in the narrow alleys. People bargained loudly. Kids laughed and shrieked. Donkeys towing carts filled with goods bumped into people on the confined pathways that Hassan had called streets.

I reminded Rachel, who easily became side-tracked shopping, of our guide's admonition. Yet, I was the one who became so delighted by a scene in front of one of the stalls that I forgot to be afraid of getting lost. A butcher was slicing a large slab of meat on the counter in front of his stand, no more than four feet wide and four feet deep, with a refrigerator taking up the entire back of the miniature butcher shop. A huge knife sharpener, glaring red with a belt that rotated to do its job, sat to his right, while another slab of meat hung from the wall to the left.

The man was clothed in a short white butcher's coat lightly stained with blood. Two stray cats – one a large black and white calico and the other a small tabby — sat eyeing the counter filled with varied sizes of dinner. Finally satisfied that I captured the perfect shot, I looked up to discover I was alone. I had fallen behind the rear guard. I froze in place, just as Hassan instructed. Within seconds, I heard Rachel's voice calling out to me. Relieved that I was back with the pack, we muddled together through the medina the rest of the morning.

Then there was the time I became disoriented on a circular path surrounded by a spectacular lush forest landscape of branches, moss, and ferns. I was on a four-week tour of Australia and New Zealand with my travel buddy, Janet, a couple of years before I planted her walking stick in the Plitvice Lakes of Croatia. We were on the west coast of the South Island of New Zealand where our group took a short walk through the Kahikatea Swamp. Following a walkway lined on each side with tall white pine trees, or *kahikatea* in Maori, most of my fellow travelers snapped an obligatory photo and continued to follow our guide, Dianne, along the slow-flowing Ship Creek. The indigenous Maori call the area *Tauparikaka*, or "parrots all walking in a row." Half-Maori herself, Dianne articulated the indigenous names with ease.

Lingering behind the rest of the group, I tried to be mindful of the habitat before taking pictures of the tree trunks covered with an astonishing variety of green ferns and moss. Even though I had acknowledged that I had an anxiety disorder before my trip to New Zealand, I never fully conquered my fear of getting lost. My therapist touted mindfulness as a way to battle my anxiety. Focusing my attention on the present moment and place, I felt as though I were walking through an alien land, perhaps a world before humans inhabited it. I lost myself in the fauna while the rest of the group was already making their bathroom stop at the entrance to the park. Suddenly, I became aware of the silence. I looked in front of me and then behind: there was no one else in sight. Since the entire walk was only one kilometer, less than a thirty-minute slow stroll, I thought I couldn't be too far from the exit. I remembered that Dianne explained that the walkway brought us back to where our van was parked.

With rising anxiety, I decided to turn around and walk back the way we had come. Since there hadn't been any forks in the pathway, I assumed I was safe from getting lost. After walking for about ten minutes, I became rattled, my rapid pulse triggering sweat even though it was quite a cold, drizzly day. Not realizing that the path was a loop, I turned around and retraced my steps in the opposite direction. I walked another five minutes before becoming disoriented and went into full panic mode.

"Hello!" I screamed at anyone in hearing range. I raised my pitch, "Hello! Dianne?" Silence.

I tried to assure myself that they wouldn't leave me here, but weren't they missing me? Why hadn't anyone come to look for me? By now it was at least twenty minutes since I had seen anyone else.

"Janeeettttt?" Janet had chosen to sit out the walk because of the wet trail, as she would do at the Plitvice Lakes. My good friend wouldn't let them take off without me. How far away could they be that they couldn't hear me?

I started to freak out, screaming loudly now. Remembering that the best chance of getting found was to remain in place, I stopped walking. Let the rescuers come to you, Hassan had advised.

"It's Faye. I'm lost! Dianne? Janet? Is anyone there?"

Finally, I heard a voice calling back to me. I quickly wiped away my tears, attempting to look calmer than I was.

After finishing the trail, everyone had visited the bathrooms, and knowing that I was busy taking photos, they all assumed I was the last one in the rest room. Janet was on her way into the ladies room to check on me when Dianne heard her name coming from the kahikatea trees. Finally, they came to my rescue. My fellow travelers teased me light-heartedly: had I walked on for about two or three more minutes in either direction I would have found them in the motor coach, waiting for me to come out of the *wharepaku*. The Maori word for bathroom doesn't quite roll off the tongue. After the ordeal, I sought solace in a stall in the FAR-eh-pah-koo, decompressing before finally joining my fellow travelers.

In the last couple of years of my tour directing career, I led several tours of "The Historic South," from Charleston, South Carolina, to St. Augustine, Florida. We don't walk much on these tours since the average age of the guests is over 65 and many of them have limited mobility.

However, the streets of historic Savannah are restricted to motor coaches, so I had to lead a brief tour on foot. I depended on my bus driver to do the navigating, but now it would be up to me. I studied the map the night before, anxious about getting lost. Like in New York, I located landmarks to assist in my wayfinding. Still, I had my smart phone in my pocket just in case.

Our driver dropped us off at the corner of Forsyth Park, and I confidently led my group to the iconic fountain. From there I had to negotiate the streets to view some of the notable homes, including the notorious Mercer Williams House, with all its bad karma. But I did well, sneaking a peek at Google maps while everyone else enjoyed the Davenport House, home to the birth of Savannah's Historic Preservation Society and the Andrew Low House, where Juliette Low started the Girl Scouts. I decided to add a site not on the itinerary: Mickve Israel, the only Gothic synagogue in the United States.

There was a group of six women from Long Island on the trip, all of them Jewish. One of the women, Charlotte, had already proven to be surly and downbeat. She insisted on saving six spaces for her ladies during group meals, causing conflict, not only with other passengers, but also with her friends who might have enjoyed meeting other people. I thought I might get on Charlotte's good side with a visit to the unique synagogue housing two of the oldest torahs in the United States.

Despite my homework, I got lost. I walked one block in the wrong direction before self-correcting with a turn on Bull Street to Monterey Square when I heard a bellowing from the back of the group.

"I thought you were a tour guide. If you don't know how to get there, I am not following you." Charlotte barked like a stereotypical New Yorker. Two of the older women traveling with her gave me an unambiguous look that signaled they were sorry.

"I know how to get there. I just missed the street. It's a very short walk." I probably explained too much.

"I'm staying right here." There was no place for Charlotte to sit, but I didn't want to get into a tussle with her.

"It's not very far, but that's your choice. You might want to go back to the park. That is where our driver is going to pick us up, and there are benches where you can sit."

There was a little bit of a "humph" before she slowly walked in the direction from which we came. I took the rest of the group to see Mickve Israel with a congregation that dates before the revolution. The neo-Gothic architecture of the 1878 building, designed by Henry G. Harrison, mirrors other houses of worship such as St. Patrick's Cathedral in New York, built around the same time. As we were appreciating the resplendent edifice, the two women who gave me the look a little earlier sauntered over to me.

"We want to apologize for Charlotte."

"You don't need to apologize for her."

They conveyed a litany of complaints against her: she was bossy, selfish, and controlling. One of her fellow travelers announced, "I will never travel with a group like this again."

When we arrived back at bus, Charlotte's two travel companions made a wide berth away from her. I need not have made the effort to visit Mickve Israel, taking the risk of getting lost. None of the ladies were exceedingly interested in seeing the historic building. However, I felt validated when a married couple on my tour, neither of whom were Jewish, told me that they went back to Mickve Israel for a tour of the interior. They very much enjoyed learning about its history and Jewish life in Savannah. It's on my long bucket list.

Most people with a fear of getting lost are also phobic about traveling, let alone leading a tour. I am atypical. It doesn't stop me from journeying to distant lands, but it does inform the way that I travel. I have learned to compensate, and, whenever I can, I leave the wayfinding to the professional guides, bus drivers and, my best friend – Siri. I am like the accountant who hires another accountant to do her taxes because it makes her too anxious to do her own. It works.

8

PICKPOCKETS

*If you don't take pocket-hankechers and watches some other cove
[chap] will.*

Charles Dickens, The Artful Dodger in *Oliver Twist*

Whether it's fair or not, I blame a lot of my insecurities on my mother, of blessed memory. She was never pickpocketed, but she was always anxious about getting mugged. My mom taught me to protect my pocketbook, especially if I were going into the city. (Don't laugh—that is what we called a purse or a handbag in New York back in the olden days.) She told me to hold the pocketbook in front of me and to keep my hand on the closure. When I first started taking students on international trips, I forgot to share my mother's sage advice.

On my second international trip as a teacher, when I finally hugged a gargoyle on top of Notre Dame Cathedral, one of our students fell victim to a pickpocket. Paul, Carolyn, Mrs. Fillmore (a parent chaperone), and I were staying in a typical small tourist hotel in Paris with our students. It had a large private dining area on the lower level where we enjoyed our breakfast buffet. The first morning, one of our students, Karen, placed her bag on the back of her chair while she and her tablemates retrieved their breakfast from the modest buffet of croissants, cheese, and assorted meats of unknown origin. We have all done that, including me, despite knowing better.

As we were readying to leave for our tour of the city of lights, Karen grabbed her purse, immediately feeling its lightness. She looked inside to find everything gone. Surprisingly, she remained calm.

"Someone took everything from my purse."

"What was in your bag, Karen?"

"My passport. Everything – my wallet and my traveler's checks."

This was 1982. Traveler's checks were still the standard form of currency for sightseers. Readers under the age of forty might not know that traveler's checks used to be the safest form of legal tender before credit cards became accepted internationally. Before leaving on a trip, people purchased checks in small denominations for the amount of money they thought they needed. Travelers were given a list of the check numbers which were to be kept safe in a place separate from the checks themselves. If the checks were stolen, unused checks were refunded. Although American Express still sells traveler's checks, I don't know why anyone would buy them since most merchants no longer accept them. Back then, however, they were the safest means of payment.

Still composed, Karen didn't remember how much money was in her wallet, but she said it was minimal. She had not yet exchanged her American Express traveler's checks for francs. Luckily, the list of her check numbers was safely concealed in her toiletry bag upstairs in her hotel room. Following caution, she had also copied her passport, storing it with the list of traveler's check numbers. Now, all we had to do was have an adult take her to the American Embassy and the American Express office, most likely a full day lost to thievery.

Anxiety may be a chemical reaction in my brain, but selfishness is a personal fault. I didn't want to miss our day in Paris due to a pickpocket. Paul and I had planned on exploring the city together. Although we were no longer in the honeymoon phase, Paris was full of romance, and I wanted to spend the day with my husband. We were starting our day at the Notre Dame Cathedral. With this self-centered justification, I waited for Carolyn or Mrs. Fillmore to come to Karen's rescue.

"Why don't I take Karen?" Mrs. Fillmore interceded. "My daughter, Susan, Greg, and Karen were going to spend the day together with me anyway. We can take care of the passport and money and have the rest of the day as we planned."

I was secretly relieved and openly grateful. Any guilt I harbored was appeased when we met up with Mrs. Fillmore and Karen later that afternoon. Their mission was accomplished, and they had a wonderful day in the city. The American Embassy was well located, close to the *Place de la Concorde* and just steps from the Louvre. After replacing the traveler's checks and the passport, the five of them enjoyed hours of shopping along the *Avenue des Champs-Élysées*, one of the world's most beautiful avenues.

The summer after my mother passed away, Rachel, a college junior at the time, had an opportunity for an internship in the People's Republic of China. A colleague of mine, David, was developing educational opportunities for American students in China, and he invited Rachel to join his daughter, Leslie, to teach English to Chinese students in a camp program in Beijing. His son, Eric, was already stationed in Beijing exploring business options for his father. After initial setbacks to the start of the program, Rachel and Leslie enjoyed their teaching until the government suddenly ended the program prematurely. With the girls having two free weeks in China, David and I decided to join them on an exploration of the country, from Beijing to Xi'an, then on to Shanghai before visiting Hangzhou and Suzhou. Finally, we would enjoy some relaxation in Macau before returning to Beijing and our flight home.

We spent a good amount of time in the Beijing Silk Market, filled with a flurry of men and women hawking their wares from silk ties to tea cups. While David was making obscenely large purchases which he planned to resell in the States, the rest of us strolled through the market in search of souvenirs. With just enough knowledge of the English language to peddle their trinkets to tourists, vendors were aggressive in their sales tactics. While Rachel enjoyed haggling in the market, I cringed every time a vendor tried to grab my attention or grasped my arm to pull me in the direction of their stall.

"Pretty lady, you want pashmina? You come. You look. You buy." The small woman with the crooked smile seized my arm and tried to lead me to a kiosk displaying glossy Chinese silks of all colors and designs.

"No, thank you. *Méiyǒu.*" Rachel tried to teach me a little Mandarin, but I sounded a bit too much like a purring cat. Although my Chinese was hopeless, I was sure the belligerent woman understood that I wasn't interested in her fake silks. Nevertheless, she persisted.

"I make you good deal. You buy." She wasn't letting go of my arm, and I was becoming uneasy.

"Mom, just ignore her and walk away." Rachel was being practical, but the woman wasn't letting go.

I felt a surge of anxiety and reacted rather abruptly: "Get your hands off of me!"

She whispered what I assumed to be a curse under her breath and finally walked in the opposite direction in search of a tourist willing to browse her silks. Becoming more anxious about the crowds of people pushing through the market, I heeded my mother's warning and clutched my small backpack, turning it to my front where I kept an eye and a hand on it.

We made a final visit to the Silk Market right before we left for home. We were searching for the souvenirs we had failed to buy on our previous forays. I bought five miniature Chinese silk brocade dress wine bottle covers for my book club ladies which were obviously fake at $3 each. I found them back home in a Chinese store for less than $2. Rachel was still in search of a teapot for herself—a small, delicately painted cup with a strainer and a lid to allow the tea to simmer. A young man approached us.

"You looking for something special? I help you find."

"We are looking for tea cups," Rachel replied.

"Come with me. I show you the most beautiful porcelain, beautiful designs. Best price."

Rachel and I followed the peddler to a booth. There, a wizened woman wearing Western clothing welcomed us, happy to flaunt her wares. While she diverted us with a demonstration of her many tea cups, I allowed the backpack to slip under my arm. Within minutes, I felt a new lightness under my shoulder. I looked down to find the bag open, camera and wallet gone.

"Fuck!" I went into full panic mode, losing all control of decorum. "Fuck, fuck, fuck, fuck, fuck." I am relatively certain everyone in the Silk Market understood that particular word.

Before I thought of anything else to say, I started shouting to no one in particular: "Please! Take anything you want, but not my camera! Just give me back my pictures." Did I imagine the scoundrel stopping, turning back, and handing me the memory card before skedaddling with my belongings?

Rachel was certain that the young man and the old woman were in cahoots. The woman distracted us while he unobtrusively opened my bag, pinching my camera and a small Louis Vuitton Chinese knock-off wallet I had purchased on an earlier venture to the market. It had 700 *yuan*, or about $100, and a couple of credit cards. Luckily, my passport was safely ensconced in a hard-to-reach pocket inside the bag.

Once my initial wrath subsided, I was able to rationalize the situation. I had lost almost 400 photos of our trip, but Rachel and Leslie had their pictures of our travels to share with me. We had two days left in Beijing to capture my own photos on Rachel's camera. Sometimes, when looking through my album, I even forget that the pictures weren't shot through my eyes. Rachel had an ATM card, and I had hidden a credit card in my toiletry bag, so we were not destitute.

I have learned ways to circumvent thievery. If I can't stop the pick-pockets, I am able to lessen the loss. I keep very little cash and only carry one credit card and an ATM card. I leave a different credit card hidden in my toiletries. When I can, I leave my passport in the hotel safe or in a difficult-to-reach pocket in my bag. I am sorry, Mom, but securing my bag well enough to stop getting robbed is just too difficult: there are very Artful Dodgers out there. Most importantly, I download my photos from my camera every night and, when I have internet access, I save them to the cloud. No one is stealing my travel photos again.

In addition to his Chinese programs, David started to organize overseas tours for students in other countries. The year after our China trip, he sweet-talked me into a whirlwind student tour of Italy, including Rome, Siena, Florence, Venice, Bologna, and Milan. I recruited a young teacher, Kim, to travel with us since I was getting old and worn-out. (I was 51!) I needed a chaperone to hang with the kids at night and make sure they were safely tucked into their beds at curfew. David enlisted his son Eric to join us as well.

I was already feeling less than good about the trip before we arrived in Italy. David had booked all the flights and held our tickets until we gathered at the airport gate. That was when I realized that Nazzi, one of my students, and I were not on the same flight as the rest of the group, and we had already missed the first leg to Paris. After much finagling, we were able to get Nazzi and me flights for later that evening. We missed the morning tour of the Roman Forum, but we caught up with everyone at the Colosseum. Still, I was less than delighted.

Since we were a small group, David had decided to utilize public transport throughout Italy, including trains, boats, and buses. Our itinerary was neither convenient nor tranquil, although it was adventurous. David was following the advice of Pope Clement XIV who wrote over two hundred years earlier: "When we're in Rome, we should do as the Romans do."

Our journey from Rome to Siena included a metro train and a public bus. We rose early, grabbed our brown-bag breakfasts and luggage and walked the short distance to the Spagna metro station. *La Metropolitana*, or the Rome metro, was our only means of transport in the city. Unfortunately, crowded transit lines, especially those frequented by tourists, are a haven for pickpockets. David thought he could avoid the likes of the Artful Dodger by wearing pocketed pants with zippers, hiding items in different compartments. As the tour manager, he carried a hefty bundle of cash for expenses, which he zipped into the bottom right pocket of his Dickies olive green work pants.

With the arrival of the A train, we all boarded the first car, jam-packed with morning commuters. David was the last to board, ensuring that all of the students made it on to the train before the doors closed. The other passengers looked at us suspiciously because we were blocking the aisles and the doors to the car with our suitcases. The lucky students who secured seats were munching on their breakfast in a bag. Locating a small space on a pole to hold on to, David wrapped his fingers around it, bag at his feet, and exchanged details about the rest of our journey with his son, Eric.

"What time does the bus leave the Rome terminal?" Eric was trying to keep up with his father's plans.

"Ten o'clock. We have plenty of time."

"Do you know where we have to go once we get to the terminal?"

"I assume there will be signs to the buses."

"Do you have a map?"

David assured his son that he was well prepared to lead us on our journey, unaware that at the same moment a skilled pickpocket had unzipped the lower compartment on his pant leg, grabbed his wad of euros, and, as the door to the train opened at a station that was not ours, exited unobtrusively. David didn't feel a thing.

After the doors closed, a weary middle-aged woman, most likely deeming us stupid Americans, spoke quietly, "He just took your money."

"Excuse me?"

"You were just robbed," she said as though she was telling him that the next stop was ours, which it was.

David reached down to the pocket to find it open, 700 euros for our trip gone with the thief. He asked the woman the same thing I wanted to ask: "If you saw it, why didn't you tell me before he got off the train?"

"I'm not starting trouble," she answered in broken English.

Not wanting to alarm the students who were too busy eating, sleeping, or chatting, David calmly announced that we were all getting off at the next stop. He told everyone to get ready to exit with their bags. No one but David, Eric, Kim, and I knew about the stolen cash.

After assuring that all of the students had safely exited the train, the four adults parlayed briefly. Relieved that this wasn't my money, I was, nevertheless, anxious that David had other means of payment for our expedition. He told me he had it covered. I offered him a sympathetic ear, although I really wanted to admonish him for not being more careful. It would do him good to develop a trickle of fear of being robbed.

There wasn't any more fleecing in Italy, but there was a lot of schlepping of big bags on public trains and boats, and even over the Rialto Bridge. We played a game of *The Amazing Race* where a group of us didn't know what a pit stop was and kept on going, not realizing the race was over. My journal says it all: "I swear I dislike the man more every day. When I see him, my skin starts to crawl." But I learned a lot from David, mostly about what not to do. I remembered him when I was developing my own tour director techniques: securing tour monies, communicating rules, and checking the details.

I was prepared for the next time when someone helped themselves to my camera, although, it was more expropriation than thievery. I was fully retired and living in my North Carolina senior adult community when I took a Christmas Markets river cruise along the Rhine River with two neighborhood friends, Scarlett and Larry Wilson. On the port stop in Strasbourg, our program director, Tim, led our small group on a morning stroll through the city center in the Alsatian region of France. We had begun our river cruise of the Rhine in Basel, Switzerland, where we were divided into three groups – red, blue, and yellow. Scarlett, Larry, and I joined about 35 other guests in the yellow group, with Tim as our guide. Tim was a doppelganger for British-born comedian John Oliver, but with a Dutch accent. He mimicked Oliver's sharp, incisive wit. Tim, who always carried a yellow flag, donned a neon orange cap to insure we never got lost as we followed him through the streets of Kaysersberg, Riquewihr, and now, Strasbourg.

The small French city on the border with Germany looks as though it is right out of a fairy tale. We walked through the Petite-France district with it canals lined with half-timbered buildings. Shops and homes alike were decorated with exquisite holiday trimmings, including oversized plush teddy bears hanging from a restaurant's windows and giant gift boxes wrapped in gold and red adorning the walls of another.

The walking portion of the tour ended in the historic center of the city at the Strasbourg Cathedral, *Cathédrale Notre-Dame de Strasbourg*, a Roman Catholic church that dominates the main square. The building grew over several centuries, creating a mix of architectural styles from the original Romanesque to the Baroque of the 17th century, but it is considered to be one of the finest examples of Gothic architecture. Tim informed us that if we wanted to visit the interior, which he highly recommended, we could do so on our own later since it was time for our boat trip through Strasbourg's canals.

Despite the miserable, wet weather, I enjoyed the slow voyage through the canals, including two water locks where they brought us up and down to the next levels of water. We glimpsed sights of the medieval architecture, timbered houses, and covered bridges. We passed the Vauban Dam, built around 1690, to protect the city from attack by raising the level of the water and flooding the city to the south.

About halfway through our ride, I placed my camera on the ledge of the window that was protecting us from the cold drizzle. It wasn't a great day for pictures, especially through the rain-soaked glass. At the end of our canal cruise, Larry, whom Scarlett affectionately calls Mr. Wilson, went back to the ship since he was feeling a little under the weather, leaving the afternoon for Scarlett and me to explore.

Scarlett is my hero and very much my opposite. She speaks frankly and doesn't take crap from anyone. She volunteers with Habitat for Humanity, actively contributes to food drives, and protests outside of Thom Tillis's office every Tuesday. Even the pandemic caused by the novel coronavirus didn't stop her, only moved her online. She makes me want to be a better person.

Scarlett and I disembarked from the boat and went in search of *nos tartes flambées*, an Alsatian pizza that the locals in this multi-lingual city, also call *flammekueche*. The thinly rolled dough, shaped in a rectangle, is topped with cheese, onions, and bacon, and cooked in a wood-fire grill. We sat down at a cozy table for two, and in a bout of apprehension of being robbed, I secured my bag underneath.

We ordered the traditional pizza to share. When the *flammekeuche* arrived, I reached for my camera for the obligatory food photo, only to find it missing. I had safeguarded my bag under the table, out of reach of pickpockets, so I deduced that I must have lost it on our walk from the tour boat to the restaurant.

After lunch, Scarlett suggested we backtrack. When we arrived at the dock where we had disembarked from the canal boat, I suddenly remembered leaving the camera on the window ledge. The boat was still there, but the niche was free of a camera, and, unfortunately, no one had turned it in. My small "point and shoot" camera was gone. Unlike my crazed reaction in the Silk Market of Beijing, this time I didn't freak out. I had only lost the photos of our morning canal ride, and those weren't very good anyway. All of the earlier pictures from our Rhine River cruise were safely stored in the Cloud, and I had my iPhone camera for the rest of the tour.

By the time I transitioned from teaching to tour directing, the smart phone had significantly changed the travel experience. It also increased the number of pickpocketing incidents. When one of our eighth-grade girls lost her iPhone in a souvenir shop at George Washington's Mount Vernon, chaperones and students alike became engrossed in the "Case of the Pilfered Phone."

Michelle was traveling with her Southern California school on their annual trip to the nation's capital, and I was their course leader, a fancy name for a tour director responsible for educating the students. The young teen lived in a world of her own, even more so than other girls her age. Her thick, dark hair was tied tightly back into a pigtail, making it easy to try on multiple sweatshirts advertising her visit to Mount Vernon and promising to keep her warm on our ghost walk that unseasonably cold spring evening.

Middle school students rarely suffer from a fear of being robbed since they believe they are infallible. I was constantly reminding them to take their phones out of their back pockets or not to leave them on the table when they were getting their food, like Karen did with her purse those many years ago. Still, Michelle carelessly laid her mobile phone on the shelf with the hoodies, only to forget about it until shortly after the bus pulled away from the long line of motor coaches in front of Mount Vernon.

As we departed Washington's home along the Potomac, I started to engage the students in a discussion of questions I had posed before their visit. "Did anyone discover what Washington's false teeth were actually made of?" I had asked the students to check out the General's false teeth in the Educational Center. Previous to their visit, they all believed the long-standing legend that they were made out of wood.

A young girl yelled out from the back of the bus: "Ivory!"

"Good. What else?"

"Teeth from dead people," said another girl sitting right behind me. Under her breath, she added, "That's really gross."

There was silence, so I offered a hint: "The last thing is a type of metal." I heard a murmuring from the back of the bus. Thinking that they were discussing possible answers, I asked someone to speak up. Michelle's seat partner did just that.

"Michelle can't find her phone!"

We were on the same journey as General Washington would have made from his main house to his townhome in what we now call Old Town Alexandria. What would have been a day's trip on horseback in colonial times was now a fifteen-minute bus ride along the Potomac on the scenic George Washington Memorial Parkway.

Unlike most student tours which are led by teachers, these middle schoolers were traveling with three volunteer parents—Miss Monica, Mr. Winston, and Miss Vicki. Miss Monica and Mr. Winston were sitting across the aisle from me, while Miss Vicki kept an eye on the students in the back. Miss Vicki, a light-skinned black woman, was a tour director's dream of a chaperone since she actually supervised the students. She instructed Michelle to walk up to the front of the bus, making sure to hold on to the back of the seats so not to fall if we made a sudden stop. As Michelle carefully walked toward me, I called Mount Vernon. The lost and found department said that no one had turned in a phone.

Since I frequently misplace my phone, I was quite familiar with "Find My iPhone," an app that allows you to locate your Apple devices. Since Michelle knew her Apple password, it was possible for me to connect to her phone on the app. I thought it was a long shot since I assumed that whoever had filched the phone was clever enough to turn off the tracking. Luckily, I was wrong. The thief was an amateur. We could see on the app that Michelle's phone was still at Mount Vernon, somewhere in the bus lane. Just as we located it, it started to move away. We had our first clue: the phone was most likely pilfered by another student on a tour of the estate. Excited by our find, we continued to track the mobile device.

As we made our way east towards the restaurant for dinner, the phone went north before going off line. Miss Monica, Mr. Winston and I were not going to give up. Our driver dropped us off at the historic corner of King Street at Il Porto Restaurant, a perfect setting for more detective work, especially considering the building's own intrigue. The colonial townhouse was originally home to a sea captain who lived there until one of his import customers had him tried and convicted for theft. At the turn of the 18th century, Madame LeCleaque turned it into a house of prostitution until one of her customers shot and killed her. After the Civil War, two elderly ladies fronted their basement wine and whiskey distillery with an antique store on the street level. The house continued its titillating history, becoming a speakeasy during the Roaring Twenties and a front for a Nazi sympathizer and spy during World War II. Now it was home to an Italian restaurant and the mystery of the stolen phone.

As everyone enjoyed their chicken parmigiana or angel hair pasta with vegetables in the private upstairs dining room, I kept an eye on the app, watching for a return of the signal. Finally, the phone came back online. It was at Pizzeria Uno in Kingstowne, about fifteen minutes away. I had an idea: I called "Tour Central" – our 24-hour lifeline for problems on the road. If the phone snatcher was traveling with the same student tour operator, a likely scenario since they often had thousands of students at Mount Vernon at the same time, Tour Central should be able to tell us what groups were currently dining at the pizzeria.

"Tour Central, this is Doug, how may I help you?"

"This is Faye Brenner with San Filipi Middle School, 09876." We had to follow a script when calling Tour Central. I assumed this might be one of the strangest calls they received.

"One of our students had her phone stolen in Mount Vernon, and we have traced the phone to Pizzeria Uno in Kingstowne. Are any of our course leaders there right now?"

I was waiting for a chuckle or an incredulous retort. It didn't come.

"Sure, hold on a minute."

Minutes later, Doug came back to the phone. "There are two groups there right now, although one is getting ready to leave for the ghost tour in Alexandria. That course leader is Ed Levi. JP Nguyen is also there with his group. Do you want their numbers?"

The course leader community is very tight. I already had both numbers in my phone. I called JP first and explained the situation. He assured me that he would talk to his chaperones. Ed didn't answer, but I left a message.

Word was spreading quickly among the students that we were having success tracing Michelle's phone. We started to draw a crowd of observers, most of them Michelle's girlfriends. I overheard her tell them that her father had warned her that the next time she lost her phone she would be grounded for life. Nobody wanted that.

JP called back first. "Their principal has talked to all of the students, and he is confident that none of them has the phone." At the same moment I looked down to see Michelle's phone on the move again, heading right to us.

"Thanks, JP. Please tell your principal we appreciate his efforts. We can see that the phone has already left the restaurant."

By then, the phone was just around the corner in Market Square, where we were scheduled to join a ghost tour later that evening. Still not hearing back from Ed, I left Miss Monica and Miss Vicki to gather their students while Mr. Winston and I ran ahead, trying to catch the thief. The victim stayed behind with her friends, trusting us to do the detective work.

I spied Wellington Watts, the proprietor of Alexandria Ghost Tours, directing traffic with the assistance of the local police. He met over forty buses of students some evenings, and tonight was one. Wellington was in stark contrast to the uniformed police with his black breeches, colonial coat and cravat, and fashionable wide-brimmed hat.

After sharing the circumstances of our investigation with Wellington, he suggested it best to wait for the group to finish its tour. Ghost guides had the freedom to change their route, but they all ended back at the square. "Find my iPhone" was still showing the phone in the area, moving along the cobbled sidewalks of Old Town, stopping to listen to tales of the supernatural. Just as a group of the perpetrator's peers were completing their tour, Ed arrived to meet them, having spent the last hour in Starbuck's across the street and not seeing my phone message. I filled him in on the crime.

Winston, Ed, and I interrogated the first group of Ted's students until we realized it wasn't anyone in their company since the phone was still walking the streets. Everyone pointed their fingers at the same person: Casey. According to his schoolmates, he had a reputation.

Finally, the phone arrived with a small group of students and their principal. After we filled in the principal with the details of our investigation, he confronted his students.

"We know one of you has a phone that doesn't belong to you. Turn it over now, and the consequences will not be as severe as if we have to search your backpacks."

Students started opening their bags. One young man pointed to a short boy with long, black wavy hair sticking out under his baseball cap. A young girl suggested that we ask Casey.

"Casey, do you have anything you want to tell us?" asked the principal.

The young boy wasn't surprised that his fellow students turned him in. He opened his backpack and took out the phone. Just then Miss Monica and Miss Vicki arrived, followed by a group of animated young teenagers excited about the ghost tour and others, especially Michelle, anxious for any information about her phone. Mr. Winston handed it to Michelle, who was saved from the wrath of her dad. It felt good playing the hero instead of the worry wart.

9

PHANTOM KILLERS

"Why do men feel threatened by women?" I asked a male friend of mine. "I mean," I said, "men are bigger, most of the time, they can run faster, strangle better, and they have on the average a lot more money and power."

"They're afraid women will laugh at them," he said. "Undercut their world view."

Then I asked some women, "Why do women feel threatened by men?"

"They're afraid of being killed," they said.

Margaret Atwood, *Writing the Male Character*

Once upon a time I came upon a cartoon about the fear of being killed, created by a webtoon designer called Starydraws. It depicted a young man snacking on French fries while his female companion sipped bubble tea.

He asks: "What's the phobia of being murdered called?"

With a look of incredulity, she replies: "Common sense."

There actually is a psychological term for the fear of being killed: Foniasophobia. *Fonias* is Greek for "killer," and we all know what a phobia is. It is common sense to be cautious, but when the fear of being killed is irrational, it can wreak havoc on your travels.

We all have the "fight or flight" response to a dangerous situation: when we become alert to a threat we are wired to protect ourselves. It makes sense to be fearful of an unfamiliar growling pit bull, but if I run away from my neighbor's fluffy-white, affable Bichon, my anxiety is unfounded and irrational. I have transformed warm-hearted Bichons into homicidal pit bulls while globetrotting around the world.

My first panic attack brought on by a fear of getting killed was on a brief overnight in Vienna on my way home from Greece. It was the summer of 2002, and I was traveling solo. My distorted imagination turned an Austrian limousine driver into a serial rapist and murderer. With a 24-hour layover in Vienna on my way home from Athens, I did something stupid — something that any well-traveled person never does — I accepted a ride from a guy hawking his service inside the airport. Sitting alone in the back seat of a black sedan, I began to regret my lack of judgement. I envisioned the rapist driver ravaging my body and throwing me into a ditch alongside the Austrian Autobahn. No one would ever know what happened to me since no one knew where I was.

As the ride became longer than I had anticipated, I gingerly asked how long the drive was to the hotel, not wanting the driver to pick up any clues that I was petrified he was planning to snuff me out.

"No worries. We are close." I don't know if he read my mind or simply thought I was anxious to relax after a long flight.

The interminable highway was comprised of two tree-lined lanes in each direction with no hint of the Viennese skyline. I murmured: "I didn't think the drive was so long."

"It's what you call the 'rush hour.'" I knew the rush hour: I had lived in New York and currently resided outside of Washington, D.C. This was not rush hour by those standards. I looked to both sides of the highway and saw no escape, only good places to hide a body.

I found comfort in the only way I knew how to relieve my anxiety: I started to sing to myself, once again relying on *The Sound of Music*. "The hills are alive, with the sound of music, with songs they have sung, for a thousand years." I mused that it was the perfect song to sing in Vienna, even if Maria Von Trapp was three-hundred miles away in Salzburg.

Eventually, I spotted the ornate spires of St. Stephen's Cathedral. Steffl, the tallest tower, looked like a gift from a higher spirit, assuring me that surely, had my driver been a murderer, he would have done the deed before we reached the cathedral. I lived to get a quick glimpse of the city before heading home the next day, feeling a bit foolish about my baseless fears.

Carolyn and I had not traveled together for twenty years when we accepted a former colleague's invitation to visit her in Sofia in 2003. After spending four days with our friend, Kathy, and her husband, the U.S. Ambassador to Bulgaria, Carolyn and I continued our globetrotting around Eastern Europe with visits to Slovenia, Hungary, and the Czech Republic, where just a year after my harrowing drive on the Austrian Autobahn, my fear of getting killed emerged on a trolley car in Prague.

We decided to attend a tourist show in Prague — "The Best of Czech Folklore," a combination of dance, music, and storytelling. A pamphlet we had picked up earlier in the day promised an "unforgettable" experience: "It is a pleasant type of folklore, offering a mix of comedy, humor, inventiveness, a good mood, and self-confidence." Although not sure how a folk show offered us self-confidence, we still decided to give it a go.

A transit map made the trip look easy: we take the number 22 from the tram station closest to our B&B near the Charles Bridge, stay on for about 25 minutes or six stops, exit at Malovanka, and walk about five minutes to the Pyramida Hotel, which was hosting the show in its grand hall. However, as we traveled west out of the city center, the types of passengers riding with us transformed from tourists and laborers heading home for the night, to seedy-looking characters. I started to wonder anxiously about our destination. Was the neighborhood safe? I calmed myself with the rationalization that if this show had been playing for over fifty years, surely tourists wouldn't continue to attend if people had been murdered on their way. After all, the Pyramida was a four-star hotel.

I couldn't think myself out of my fear. Carolyn was oblivious to my increasing anxiety, and I saw no reason to share my trepidation. I was afraid that I might appear prejudiced, sneering at these men because they weren't as well dressed as we were. As we finally exited the tram, I walked side-by-side with my long-time travel buddy in a neighborhood that had not yet become gentrified. We entered the Pyramida Hotel, with its modern, pyramid-shaped concrete structure, an archetype of the Brutalist architecture of the mid-twentieth century.

By the time the folk show started, my apprehension subsided, and we enjoyed the performance with an audience mostly comprised of tourists who had safely arrived at the theater in their chartered motor coaches. As everyone else boarded their buses at the end of the performance,

I convinced Carolyn into returning to our bed and breakfast by taxi, avoiding another panic attack on the public trolley. I feigned fatigue, embarrassed by my foniasophobia.

Three years later, on a trip to "Sunny Portugal" with my adventurous travel buddy, Susan, we were strolling along a beach on a glorious afternoon in Alvor, a small fishing village in the southernmost region of Portugal. We stumbled upon a sign advertising an excursion on a traditional Portuguese fishing boat for just 15 euros. A young, ruddy-looking man explained that the captain was returning in about an hour and asked us to come back later. After enjoying a banana milk shake on the beach, Susan and I returned to the dock to find "the mate... [a] mighty sailing man" and "the skipper brave and sure...for our three-hour tour."

Captain Toby looked more like a model out of *GQ* than a skipper of a fishing boat, albeit one that was for tourist expeditions rather than trawling. He wore a grey tank lined with a hefty gold chain with just enough chest hair exposed to be sexy rather than grubby. He was fine-looking from the top of his bald head, accented with dark sunglasses, to his bare feet, blanketed by his dark jeans. He looked no more like a rapist or a murderer than the innocent limousine driver in Vienna. My panic materialized when I grasped the situation: Susan and I were the only ones going out on the small vessel with the skipper and Captain Toby, who suddenly became a pit bull with his bull terrier companion, each with a robust drive for prey, and we were the game.

Had I been alone or with almost anyone other than Susan, I would have made a cockamamie excuse why I no longer wanted to go sailing, but Susan insisted that I was not going to ruin an unexpected opportunity for an adventure because of my unfounded paranoia. Embarrassed, I climbed aboard the small open vessel with the two *marujo*, or seamen, and my fearless friend.

I had seen a boat just like this one in my family's volume P of *The World Book Encyclopedia*, the omnipresent resource for information in middle-class homes of the mid-twentieth century. Our sixth-grade curriculum required us to choose a country to research for most of the school term – I chose Portugal — submitting the facts, history, culture, and pictures pasted on colored construction paper held together with steel rings. As part of the project, we were required to write letters to request more information from tour agencies and the international version of a chamber of commerce. The travel brochures offered me numerous photographs of the iconic Portuguese fishing boat which had suddenly become the site of a possible double rape and homicide.

As Captain Toby turned on the motor to proceed out of the marina, I pulled my legs up to my chest and grabbed my knees to stop their shaking. I looked out at the distant ocean, breathing in the scent of the sea. I practiced my relaxation breathing techniques until Captain Toby slowed our vessel, coming to a complete halt in front of a grotto. This was it. No amount of deep breathing was going to alleviate my anxiety. We were sailing into the cavern where the men planned to rape us, throw us to the floor of the boat, and drive out to sea to dump our bodies.

Suddenly, our captain became our tour guide. "We are stopping here to get a better look at the entrance to Boca de Inferno. If we had more time we could get closer, but for now, you can enjoy the remarkable rock formations." The coastline of Cascais is lined with cliffs formed by limestone eroded by the force of the Atlantic Ocean.

"Some people have said that they hear ghoulish sounds coming from inside the cavern, the 'Mouth of Hell' in English. Legend has it that a sorcerer fell in love with a beautiful woman, captured her and locked her inside his castle that once stood on this spot. When a gallant gentleman attempted to save the maiden, the evil sorcerer created a tremendous ocean storm, swallowing the two of them up into the waters. If we could get close enough, you might still hear their screams."

"You've got to be kidding me," I thought. "The two of us are going to die in the Mouth of Hell!"

We sailed away. I took a deep breath, relaxing in the knowledge that, if they were going to murder us, they missed the perfect scene for the crime.

By then, Susan was conversing with Captain Toby, as she was wont to do. Our skipper was married with a baby daughter, Lila. Originally from London, he had visited the Algarve and fell in love. He moved here and opened his boating expeditions for tourists. Illogically, knowing he had a wife and a baby put the final cap on my anxiety, even though John Wayne Gacy was twice married and had two biological children. I managed to relax and enjoy the rest of our sailing adventure. As we pulled back into the dock, Toby's wife greeted us, holding baby Lila in her hands. Susan and Toby exchanged email addresses, and, to this day, they keep in touch. As far as I know he still hasn't murdered anyone.

Perhaps my anxiety over a boat ride with two strange men or a tram ride with dodgy people arose over common sense, but, in both instances, I felt foolish having almost surrendered to my fear. My experience in Casablanca, on the other hand, was a bit of a different story. Our tour director, Hassan, scared us into staying in our hotel, although he was more concerned with potential harassment than murder when he told us that it was not safe to walk around at night, especially for unaccompanied women. Like our later sojourn in the Fés medina, Hassan was simply trying to keep us all safe.

"Although it is rare for a man to make physical contact," he told us, "you might be targets of verbal abuse or purse-snatching." He cautioned us that the best option was not to go out. Since none of us had our bags, Hassan accompanied our group across the street to a sundry shop for any items we might need. Before we returned to the hotel he advised us that, if we do go out, we must ignore anyone threatening us. "Just keep walking in the opposite direction," he said.

I recalled a much earlier warning against men in Italy when, as teenage girls, we were taught to shout *"Basta!"* at unwanted attention. I didn't think the Arabic *Kafia!* was sufficient, so I was determined to keep my twenty-something daughter and me inside the hotel after our chaperoned shopping spree. Since our hotel was hosting a gala New Year's Eve celebration for its guests that night, there was no reason to go anywhere else.

Dressed in the jeans and an orange embroidered Indian-style tunic that I had worn on the plane, I accompanied Rachel to the party. She put on a flowered fuscia-colored tank blouse that she had in her carry-on, dressing it up with a white camisole. Our small group of tourists was easily distinguishable from the rest of the New Year's Eve merrymakers in their sparkling gowns and black suits. There were even a couple of men in tuxedos. Our unintentional casual attire didn't make the drinks any less strong nor the food any less tasty. We reveled in the opportunity to celebrate after two days of travel and lost bags. Besides, the well-endowed belly dancer made us all forget the difficult journey for a while. As I watched her generous belly jiggle in all directions, I wondered, "How does she do that?"

I left Rachel at the New Year's Eve party at the hotel restaurant and went up to my room to go to sleep. After changing into my pajamas and getting under the covers, I was struck by a frightful case of anticipatory anxiety. I had a vision of Rachel being kidnapped from the hotel. I closed my eyes and tried to change the picture to a more affirming one. Instead, I imagined Rachel leaving the hotel with some new friends, only to be accosted or murdered on the street. I felt the familiar churning of my stomach, the collywobbles, as I sprang out of bed and put my clothes back on. As I exited the elevator to the lobby, I found Rachel saying goodnight to some of the other party goers. I lied, or at least told a half truth. I said I couldn't sleep so I came back to see how the celebration was going. With my daughter safely by my side, we went back to our room.

Like so many of my specious phobias, my fear of being killed extends to my family, especially my children. That New Year's Eve was the night my collywobbles turned into a full-fledged anxiety attack. There was no basis for my apprehension. Rachel wasn't galivanting through the streets of Casablanca; she was downstairs at a party with others in our group. Yet, the only way I could ease my rapidly beating heart and calm my breathing was to be reunited with her. This went beyond the conventional stereotype of a neurotic Jewish mother. It might be time to get help.

10

CALAMITIES

*The Earth is God's pinball machine and each quake, tidal wave,
flash flood and volcanic eruption is the result of a TILT that occurs
when God, cheating, tries to win free games.*
                    Tom Robbins, *Even Cowgirls Get the Blues*

Astraphobia, the fear of natural events, is most common in children and
dogs, not grown-ups like me. Dogs are afraid of thunder because they
don't understand what is causing the reverberant sound. We can lessen
their anxiety with a thunder shirt or loud music to drown out the threatening noise. Neither of my canine companions, however, are bothered
by thunder, although neither will brave the rain to do their business.
My daughter, on the other hand, developed an extreme fear of storms at
summer camp at six years old.

My two children and I spent thirteen summers at camp. When I
started as the camp's drama specialist, Rachel spent the day with other
staff members' children and their counselors and the nights with me.
Joshua was old enough to be a camper. Eventually, Joshua and Rachel
would both become staff members, but until then, every summer was a
vacation to them.

It was our first summer at camp, and I was rehearsing an abridged
production of *Joseph and the Amazing Technicolor Dreamcoat* in the
outdoor theater when the sky suddenly darkened, and the wind
quickly intensified. An announcement came over the camp's speaker
system.

"Attention campers and staff. We have a serious threat of dangerous weather. If you can safely get to the dining hall, please do that immediately. If not, and you are in a safe position, remain there."

The theater had a small backstage area with two small windows that shut, so we stopped rehearsal and took refuge between two wooden walls. I didn't know it at the time, but the staff brats, as everyone called them, were doing arts and crafts in the small shack that stood on the way down Killer Hill, so-called since it was a steep, long climb between the pool and lake and the rest of the camp. The counselors had the little ones hiding under the tables, in itself traumatic to a six-year-old.

In the meanwhile, the swim staff decided it was best to send everyone up to the dining hall. As the children followed their counselors up the hill, a large tree snapped. A falling limb hit Jordana, one of the younger girls, slashing her forehead.

Since the arts and crafts shack offered not only protection, but also running water, one of her counselors brought Jordana into the cabin to wash her up and attempt to curtail the bleeding. Although her cuts seemed to be minor, the blood was steadily streaming from her forehead. Rachel, who was hiding under the table for safety from the gale-force winds, had her fears validated when she saw blood-soaked Jordana. As the winds diminished, the staff children, Jordana, and the four counselors in the arts and crafts shack, walked past the empty theater on their way to the safety of the dining room, not noticing those of us taking refuge backstage.

The first thing Rachel did when she entered the dining hall was to look for me. She wanted her mommy, and, when neither of her counselors could find me, she panicked. No one knew where the drama kids were, although it made sense that we were still in the theater. This was 1989. I didn't have a cell phone or a walkie-talkie, but we stayed put, thinking it the best way to avoid the nasty weather.

Later that day, I learned we had experienced a microburst, a column of air, usually about two miles wide, that pushes down to the ground, causing significant damage. All I knew, while hiding in the theater, was that it was horribly windy, and it was my responsibility to keep the campers safe. I trusted my children's counselors to do the same. Finally, when the storm passed, I walked the campers up to the dining hall.

Rachel ran to me, crying and hugging and screaming at me all at once. "Where were you? Why didn't you come to the dining hall like everyone else?" At six, her questions were probably a little less well-formed.

Eventually, knowing we were all safe and the storm was over, she calmed down. But a second storm that summer solidified her fear. This time it was lightning rather than wind. The campers and counselors were hunkered down in their cabins waiting for the thunderstorm to pass.

Everyone knew the drill: move to safe shelter, stay there until at least a half hour after the last sound of thunder, avoid electrical equipment, and stay away from water since it can act as an electrical conductor. I can only assume that one of our male counselors didn't consider his battery-operated transistor radio electrical equipment, but, when lightning struck, it threw him across the cabin, knocking his head on the wall before he slumped on to one of the meager camp beds. Besides superficial burns, he was fine. Even though Rachel didn't witness the force of the lightning, stories spread like the game of telephone, and my daughter's fear of storms was ingrained in her young psyche.

Back home later that year, our family of four was shopping in a big box store when a fierce rain fell on the metal roof, making a deafening sound.

"Mommy, please, we have to leave."

Her father had no patience for her fears. "It's just raining. Nothing is going to happen to you."

She began to shake. She started to cry. "We have to go home."

We went home and called a therapist. Rachel's weather phobia lasted a decade.

The following year I was promoted to program director and, eventually, in 1993, I was hired as the executive director of the camp and retreat center. The summer of 2000 brought several calamities, natural and man-made.

It was a Friday morning in August. I was taking a shower in the narrow stall in my geodesic dome that I called home for the summer when I was interrupted by a fervent knocking on my door. I threw on a towel and opened the screen to find two of our international support staff covered with blood. It wasn't theirs. Martin, our night watchman from Slovakia, explained that three of our girls, all from Poland, were driving down to the lower camp when a deer ran in front of them. Danka lost control, swerving off the winding road. The van was only designed for one passenger, and Agnieszka wasn't in a proper seat.

"Aga got thrown from the van and hit her head on the doorjamb." Agnieszka used the nickname for the ease of us Americans. The blood was hers.

He had already called an ambulance, so I quickly dressed and drove to the local hospital.

"Agnieskza was lucky," the doctor explained. "If she had hit her nose just a few centimeters to the right, her airway would have collapsed, and it could have been fatal. She broke her cheek bone, and she will need plastic surgery. But she will recover."

I had been back to camp for less than an hour when I heard a voice on my walkie-talkie. It was my food manager, Liora.

"Faye, Rica just fell off of the loading dock. I think she might have broken something. She's on her way to the hospital."

Our dining hall at camp was kosher, which meant we were required to have someone to ensure that we comply with the Jewish dietary laws. Rica was one of our *mashgiachim*, or supervisors. I placed both of my hands over my eyes, holding them tightly closed. This couldn't be happening! Then I breathed out a big sigh. Rica could take care of herself. She was tenacious. After the ER cast her broken foot, she returned to the kitchen and finished preparing Shabbat dinner for the campers and staff.

By now it was getting close to our Friday evening service. Seeing all the middle schoolers dressed in their Shabbat whites brought me a tranquility that had been missing all day. Our campers sat on wooden benches in the bucolic setting singing *L'cha Dodi*: "Come, my beloved, to greet the bride and let us welcome the presence of Shabbat."

The calm was broken when I looked up to see Jhanna, my assistant, running toward me. I didn't wait for her to reach the pavilion, primarily because, whatever was the problem, the campers needn't know.

"There was a fire in the dining hall," Jhanna whispered, just in case anyone else was in hearing distance. She explained that it was a small fire and that she was able to put it out with Martin's help. "Can you call 911?"

I called the fire department, but, since the fire was already extinguished, I asked them not to use their sirens. I didn't want to alarm the campers. The fire truck arrived in silence, meeting us in front of the dining hall. I could still hear the sound of the campers and counselors singing. After examining the remains of the blaze, one of the firemen walked over to me.

"You had a small electrical fire, but your system is antiquated and really needs to be replaced. You were lucky this time, but it is an accident waiting to happen."

I assured him that our maintenance team would take care of it. He still looked concerned.

"Are you aware that there is a tornado watch for this evening?"

It wasn't raining, and the clouds didn't seem ominous. Rachel, who was now a counselor-in-training, had finally outgrown her fear of weather, so I avoided my motherly concern for her. But I was in charge of over four hundred other children.

"No," I answered sheepishly. I was unsettled about the fire and still distressed from the morning accidents.

"You need to get these kids inside – someplace safe."

There was no tornado-proof place in camp. I instructed the counselors to take their campers to our main building – the *Ulam*. The Hebrew word means "porch," which describes the wooden structure at the middle school camp more appropriately than a "building" since an entire side was merely screened. A big wind might be able to knock it over, let alone a rapidly rotating column of air. It would have to do. Soon after the rains began, so did the wind, but, fortunately, the tornado never took shape.

After sending all of the campers to their cabins, I returned to my modest abode in the geodesic dome just across from the dining room and called my dear friend and teacher colleague, Ron.

"Ron, I can't do this anymore. Please help me get back into the schools." I would have a job teaching at my former high school by the end of the summer.

I not only left the camp that summer, but my husband and I decided to leave each other. Sometime that same summer, Paul came up to camp for a visit. He was starting to visit less frequently, so I knew something was looming. He was distant, more so than usual. After a lot of probing, he confessed. "I have been thinking about us a lot. Maybe you are right. Maybe we should take some time apart. Maybe we should get separated." I agreed. By that spring I was an independent woman.

Rachel was off to college, and Josh was starting his life as an adult after graduating from college. I didn't stop worrying about them, but it was easier not knowing what they were up to. As Rachel grew out of her fear of storms, I was faced with numerous natural disasters while globe-trotting that might challenge even the seasoned traveler.

Although I was an anxious child, I wasn't afraid of such natural events as thunderstorms, like my daughter. My lack of fear continued well into adulthood until my 2004 trip to Japan. Honored to be chosen as a Fulbright Memorial Scholar, I joined 200 American educators for a three-week study program examining the Japanese educational system, as well as its history and culture.

Jet-lagged from our long journey, I hadn't had much sleep the first night in Tokyo. A group of us wanted to visit the famous Tsukiji fish market. In order to experience the tuna auction that happened every morning before sunrise, I set my alarm for the absurd hour of 3:30 am. I was under the sheets asleep when I felt my bed move, more like *The Exorcist* than *The Quake*. At first I wasn't sure if I were dreaming or awake until I felt a second tiny tremble. There were no alarms, no announcements, and no one but me was frightened by the seismic activity. Unnerved, I called the front desk.

"*Konnichiwa*, do you speak English?" We had been required to learn a couple of Japanese phrases before beginning our program. I said "hello," although this greeting was usually for mid-day and not the middle of the night. I was surprised that I remembered even that considering my angst at the moment.

The calm voice on the other end answered: "Of course, how may I help you, Miss Brenner?" This was a fancy-schmancy hotel if they called me by name.

"I thought I felt the building shake."

"That was just an earthquake."

Just an earthquake? Who says it was "*just* an earthquake"? I took a moment to respond while I digested what he had said.

"What should I do?" I asked, ready to run for an exit or jump into my bathtub on the twentieth floor of the Hotel New Otani, consistently rated as one of the best hotels in Tokyo.

"Nothing, go back to sleep."

"How am I supposed to go back to sleep?"

"Our hotel is very safe, Miss Brenner. It is earthquake resistant, and we just had a minor tremble. It barely registered a 5 at the epicenter. It is nothing."

I had never lived through an earthquake before, although this was not "the Big One." But I felt the earth move under me, and, for a brief moment, I was scared out of my wits. When the shaking stopped, I became less agitated. I was still too afraid to take Tylenol PM just in case I had to run to safety if there were another, stronger quake. Eventually, sleep displaced anxiety. I didn't know that a tremor occurs in Japan at least every five minutes, and each year there are up to 2,000 quakes that can be felt. I had felt this one.

That was not the only natural disaster on our Japanese adventure. We had not one, but two typhoons while we were in Tokyo. Super Typhoon *Ma-on* descended upon us just a couple of days after the earthquake, followed by Typhoon *Tokage* a day before our departure almost three weeks later. When our group leader, Reico, informed us that our day trip to Kyoto was cancelled in anticipation of the typhoon, I became quite concerned. I was a well-educated, fifty-year old woman, and I was absolutely clueless about typhoons. I thought they were either like monsoons since the two words sounded similar, or tornadoes because they both started with a "T." Either I wasn't listening in elementary school when we studied weather, or the teacher didn't think her students would ever be in the Pacific, and, therefore, she deemed an understanding of typhoons useless knowledge. Refusing to embarrass myself, I hid my ignorance and unease until, while planning a typhoon party, a primary school teacher explained it was simply semantics: what we call a "hurricane," people in the Northwest Pacific call a "typhoon."

We name our hurricanes in the United States differently than Japan names their typhoons. Japan gives theirs two labels, a number and a name. We experienced typhoons 22, named *Ma-on* for a mountain in Hong Kong that means "horse saddle" in English. Typhoon 23 was called *Tokage*, or Lizard. We name our hurricanes like we name our children, but in annual alphabetical order: 2004 brought us Alex, Bonnie, and Charley and, finally, Otto before the end of the year.

Since *Ma-on* wasn't expected until late afternoon, we had time to explore Tokyo on our own that morning, free of lectures and field trips. A group of us visited the Tokyo National Museum before finding a liquor store to stock up for the storm. Our timing was a little off when, as we walked back to the hotel carrying bottles of wine and saké, *Ma-on* poured down, drenching us from head to toe. Almost three inches of rain pelted downtown Tokyo in less than an hour. Metro stations were overwhelmed with water cascading down the subway stairs. Our umbrellas were useless against the typhoon's winds.

I was scared and sought refuge from the storm. Luckily, the liquor store wasn't too far from the hotel, and we all made it back just a little worse for wear. Returning to the safety of my room, I was changing out of my sodden socks and shoes when the sound of the fierce wind rammed the large picture window that looked out on to a traditional Japanese garden. Now I knew why they called it *Ma-on*. It might as well have been a saddled horse trying to break through the glass. I tried to appease my anxiety with reason. If the Hotel New Otani withstood earthquakes, it also kept me safe from a typhoon. My attempt at rationalization didn't appease my anxiety. The solution was in the heavy wet bags we had just lugged home – saké, and a lot of it.

Unlike *Ma-on*, Typhoon *Tokage*, the deadliest storm that decade, simply sideswiped us on our last day in Japan. Having already endured one typhoon, I was cocky. At least now I knew what was coming. Hotel staff were even more assured since this was their tenth typhoon that year. The now familiar sound of the wind on the windows serenaded me as I packed for our departure the next morning. Our program ended that evening with a "*Sayonara* Buffet," where we were joined by our group leaders and guest lecturers. We were too busy celebrating the end of our program to take note of the news of landslides and flooding in Western Japan. 95 souls lost their lives in that storm. A fear of natural calamities is not unfounded.

The Tokyo earthquake was my first rodeo. My second seismic activity was just around the corner from home. No one really expects an earthquake in Virginia, but in the summer of 2011 a 5.8 magnitude quake rocked the nation's capital. Its epicenter was about ninety miles south in the small town of Mineral.

Although I had led tours in my Old Town neighborhood, there is always more to learn. It's beneficial to observe how other tour guides present information, so that morning I looked forward to joining Tammy, our fearless local leader, on an exploration of the colonial city with visits to Christ Church, where George Washington had his own pew; Ramsey House, a reconstruction of one of the first homes; and Market Square, a Saturday morning market since 1749. Our tour ended across the way at Gadsby's Tavern.

The 1792 City Tavern is an historic inn where Washington celebrated his birth night. The General often took his meals here. Locals congregated in the main dining room to learn the latest news. Presidential candidate Thomas Jefferson awaited the 1800 election results in the tavern, spending $5.50 for his dinner and lodging and offering a 75-cents tip to his enslaved waiter. He celebrated his inauguration in the ballroom upstairs. At the end of our tour, we finished with lunch at the tavern, now a restaurant serving colonial and contemporary foodstuffs.

We had just finished our salad with Sally Lunn bread, a slightly sweet yeast bread named for an 18th century English woman. Our codfish, chicken salads, and Monte Cristo sandwiches were being served at our long wooden table in the back room when it felt as though the building was caught in a wave, followed by an enormous boom. We don't think earthquake in the nation's capital: we think bomb. At least that is what I thought.

I was flabbergasted that the tour guides continued to eat as though nothing had happened. As everyone talked over each other, Alex, the only other person who stopped to consider what just happened, walked up to a window. I joined him in his concern. The hostess saw us looking out into the street for answers and explained that we had just experienced a small earthquake. The waves of the quake were replicated in my stomach. Alex and I returned to our tables where our peers were still munching on their lunch and *kibitzing* with each other. Their lack of curiosity made me more relaxed. So, just like I went back to bed in Tokyo, I went back to my chicken salad.

The wait staff hurried our meals and checks. When we finally walked out of the tavern on to Queen Street, we were met by people standing in the street, safely away from the sidewalk. Many of the nearby buildings had been evacuated, including the Gadsby Tavern Museum, which was part of the same colonial structure as the restaurant. Those on the sidewalk were looking up at the tavern's roof. My eyes followed theirs to the cracked chimney that was leaning down toward the street. While we were enjoying our rum-laced banana bread pudding, most everyone else on the block had been evacuated.

Fearful of a collapse, we moved away from the historic structure and dispersed, not yet understanding the scale of destruction to sites that we often visit, including the Washington Monument, which was closed on and off for five years after the earthquake, and the Washington National Cathedral, where repairs were estimated to reach $25 million. My recovery was swift, but the nation's capital took a long time to heal.

Earthquakes, microbursts, and typhoons made me apprehensive, but driving in snow and ice causes panic. No one loves to drive in bad weather, but I have skidded enough times to choose to stay home rather than risk sliding down an icy road.

My book club was in our sixth year when we decided on a winter retreat to choose our reading for the year. It was January 2007, and we chose a lovely country inn in Berkeley Springs, W. Virginia. The warm, natural mineral springs of the area gave rise to several spas. After a day of discussing books and enjoying a delicious dinner at the inn, we planned a morning of spa treatments at the historic Roman Bath House. The weather report called for snow and possible icy conditions later that day, so we set out to return home as soon as we finished our morning massages.

I was driving my Prius, not a great drive on snow and ice. As we rode into the North American Ice Storm, I had a firm grip on my steering wheel. I stopped talking to my passengers in order to concentrate on the road. I started to panic each time I felt the wheels of the car slide to the side. There were four other women from my book club in the car with me, and they wanted to get home. I tried, but fear won out. Twenty minutes from Alexandria, I announced that I could not drive one more mile. I exited the road, knowing that the Fairview Park Marriott was situated at its end. If my book club friends were angry, they didn't show it, at least not yet.

I felt a responsibility for failing to get us home, so I announced that I'd take care of everything. When I stepped up to the front desk I explained that I needed rooms for five women. First, I was relieved that I was safely shielded from the snow and ice in the hotel and second, that they had available rooms. That was until the desk agent revealed the rate: $400 for each room. They were gouging us, raising their prices dramatically and taking advantage of those of us trying to escape a dangerous ice storm. I started to cry.

"I cannot drive any further, and I made my friends stop here. I can't ask them to pay that kind of money. That's ridiculous." Even if we doubled up, that's $200 a person plus all the fees hotels add on to the bill.

"That is the available rate."

"We are not paying $400 for one night. If we have to, we will just sleep in the lobby."

I walked away, feeling the same sense of panic I always have when I feel out of control, even worse when I think I am disappointing my friends with whom I had just spent a delightful two days in the mountains of West Virginia.

I was in tears when I made it back to the small group of women waiting for me in the well-appointed lobby, unaware that it might be our bedroom for the night. We were not the only ones that the storm forced off the road. There was another woman sitting in the lobby, looking quite despondent. She overheard me explaining the quoted rates, and she piped in that she couldn't afford to stay there either and was hoping to get back on the road shortly.

As we were discussing what to do, the young man at the front desk walked over.

"I called my manager, and, since this is an emergency situation, he told me that I can give you the rooms for $150. Will that work?"

It most certainly did. We took three rooms, and we waited out the storm with drinks, food, and a good night's sleep. One of the book club ladies, Karen, wondered if I found a new way to get a discounted rate: tears.

Still another natural disaster struck when Susan and I visited Vietnam and Cambodia in 2011. When we revealed our intention to visit Vietnam we were often greeted with the same question: Why? Like most people my age, I had grown up watching the Vietnam War on television. I remember not only the onslaught of bullets, but also the assaulting rain. I had a vivid image of filthy young men trudging through the jungle, boots tramping in the mud. But we had pulled out of Vietnam thirty-six years earlier, and I had heard captivating tales of the intriguing country and its people.

Susan and I joined a group of American travelers for a two-week adventure filled with delectable foods, magnificent sites, friendly people, and an abundance of rain. We had not realized that we signed up for a journey to Southeast Asia in the monsoon season, but the floods that autumn of 2011 were anything but typical. A relentless cycle of storms had left much of Vietnam and parts of Cambodia under water, flooding homes and streets and causing numerous landslides. The Mekong Delta had the worst flooding in eleven years, exacerbated by the slow onset and continuing rains from September to December.

We arrived in Cambodia on October 30. Phnom Penh and Siem Reap were free of rain, although the ground had already been saturated. The cities were relatively protected from the flooding, but the rural areas of the Mekong Delta were overwhelmed. When we arrived at *Tonie Sap*, the Great Lake, I glimpsed the first signs of the devastation. People had abandoned their meager wooden homes for higher ground. We were scheduled to visit a local school that provides a free education to children living in poverty, but it was closed due to the flooding and stayed shut for over a month after we were long gone. There was no way for the children to get to their classes.

On one of the rare sunny days, we stopped at the home of a three-generational Cambodian family. Three women, one of whom was the matriarch of the family, sat on a small wooden platform with six children, ranging in age from infant to young teen. Scantily protected from the elements by a thin blue tarp tented above them, they smiled despite our intrusion. They were surrounded by water, their home made accessible by wooden ramps hastily built above the rising flood. Almost 180,000 Cambodian homes were lost in the floods of 2011. But this day, with the sun shining and smiles beaming, this family opened their home to us, as proud as if they lived in the Taj Mahal. I was humbled and concerned.

The monsoon rains didn't hit us directly until our second day in Ho Chi Minh City on an excursion to the Cu Chi Tunnels. It was as if my friends' warnings about visiting Vietnam were, in a bizarre twist of reality, being realized. As we walked out of a barrack that was primarily underground, we were pelted with rain. The earth had already been turned into mud, saturated by the prior downpours. Floodwaters had created a ten-foot-wide stream traveling through the woods that hid the tunnels underneath. As we attempted to find shelter, the sound of bullets echoed through the rain. I was in Vietnam, running in the rain and people were trying to shoot me. I tried to play tricks on my imagination, making believe that I was on a movie set reenacting a battle along the front, safe from the fake bullets which, actually, were coming from a firing range where visitors shot M16s and other war-related firearms. I wasn't sensing their loving of peace, independence, and happiness that the brochure claimed was the mission of our visit.

It did stop raining long enough for me to defy claustrophobia down in the tunnels.

That was the beginning of the rains that never let up. Back in New York, my father was getting anxious about the flooding. I posted a video on Facebook of us walking through six inches of water at the Citadel.

He commented on my post: "You shouldn't be walking in that water."

He was worried what else might be wafting in that water. When I wrote him an email to assuage his concern, he begged me to be careful. I defied my mother by going down into the Hasmonean tunnels and riding the Egged bus in Israel. Lying again, I promised to stay out of the water as much as possible.

There was no way to avoid the flooding in Hoi An. Our first stop was the Quan Cong Temple where spontaneous waterfalls interrupted our walk from one open room to the next. An umbrella wasn't going to keep me dry, so I bought a rain poncho for 20,000 *dong*, or one dollar, from one of the street vendors. That poncho became indispensable throughout our journey.

The following day was on our own. Susan and I had signed up for one of our favorite types of excursions – a cooking class. This one started with a visit to the market, followed by an expansive Vietnamese meal cooked on board a boat.

When we arrived at our designated meeting place, we were told that the flooding and continuing rains made it too dangerous to sail out on the water. However, they also had a kitchen for cooking classes on land. First, we would ride to the market and then continue to the well-covered kitchen pavilion.

"Can you ride a bicycle?" asked our guide and cooking instructor.

I thought this a bizarre question since we were obviously unfit women between middle age and of advanced years, and it was raining cats and dogs.

I had fallen off a bicycle about a quarter of a century ago, and I had not gotten back on one since. "No, is there any other way to go?"

"Yes, of course, we have scooters. We will ride with you on a motor bike."

Locals moved around the city on pedicabs, bicycles, and scooters, none of which would keep us dry. I was all in for the scooter when, in another curious twist, Susan answered, "I'll ride a bike."

"What?" I exclaimed. "You are going to ride a bicycle? Are you nuts?"

"No, I like to ride."

"It's pouring."

"That's okay. It will be fun."

I don't know why she ever thought it might be fun to ride a bicycle in the crowded streets of Hoi An alongside scooters and pedestrians, all the while being drenched by a deluge. We were joined by a Filipino couple from Australia, she on a scooter and he, bravely, also on a bicycle.

Our guide, Dong, gave me a small helmet to protect my head in case we crashed, and, as I sat behind him covered in my 20,000-*dong* poncho, I held on for dear life. Since there was no way to keep our feet dry, we gave into the water and simply wore flip flops. Susan, in her sturdy yellow poncho that she had smartly brought from home, smiled as she dropped her bag into the front basket on the bike, and we were off on our adventure.

I don't know how we were expected to keep together: two plodding bicycles and two swift scooters. The bicycle was difficult to control on the wet pavement, and Susan quickly fell back from us. We backtracked, finding her distraught. We were close to the market, so, after a brief respite, Susan agreed she was able to make it the rest of the short distance.

After touring the market and picking up ingredients for our cooking class, we returned to our different modes of transport.

"I can't do this. Is there any other way?" Susan asked after a brief attempt to ride again.

"Of course. The four of you wait right here. I will ride the bicycle back to a garage and call my wife so she can join us with her motorbike." Dong's wife arrived on her scooter about the same time he returned. Susan hopped on with Dong while his wife drove me the rest of the way. By the time we arrived at the cooking class in a nearby village, the gentleman on the bike was spent, huffing and puffing, and needing a bit of a sit-down before we were able to start cooking.

After the class, Dong and his wife dropped us off in the center of Hoi An to shop. As we were riding on the back of the scooters, we spotted people wading through calf-high waters in the middle of the street. In deference to my dad and our tired, wet feet, we found a piece of dry land where we relaxed over a cup of Vietnamese coffee and mousse cake in a small café before returning to the hotel.

Rising waters continued to cause mounting concern the next morning. As we departed from our lovely hotel in Hoi An, we were met by a swollen stream running down the street. Pieces of debris floated along the muddy water. Most of us were feeling a sense of dread. As the driver navigated the floods, I heard whispers from the group.

"Oh, God!"

"I've never seen anything like this."

"We are not going to make it."

Since the motor coach sat high, it was able to navigate the roads that were inaccessible to scooters and bicycles. Still, we watched the water rising above the tires. Once we made it out of the city, I breathed a little easier. The roads were wet, but not flooded. When we arrived in the charming city of Hue along the Perfume River, the water once again rose up the bus.

When we finally reached our next lodging, the flood waters had overwhelmed many of the roads. The benches outside the hotel's restaurant sat under water with a single piece of metal rising above to let us know there was something underneath. We sat down for lunch, and as we ate our deliciously crisp spring rolls, or *cha gio*, we looked out on a large lagoon that used to be a field, with water creeping up the length of the trees.

Our ride to dinner that night on a cyclo, a three-wheeled taxi with a seat for two in the front, was cancelled, and we hunkered down in the hotel, watching as mother nature wreaked havoc across the city. The rains never stopped. They paused enough the following day for us to have our one-hour cyclo ride, our single-seated front carriage covered in brightly colored tarps to protect us from the light rain. Between the plastic and my rain-covered glasses, I didn't see much on the ride to dinner, but our meal in the Citadel was worth the trip.

Bad weather can ruin a holiday. Yet, despite the once-in-a-decade flooding, I never thought our trip to Cambodia and Vietnam a disaster. The rain was a part of the experience. Although the Mekong Delta often receives more rain in one month than we experience in a year, this rain was extraordinary. Over 150 people in Cambodia and Vietnam died in the flooding of 2011. While we were traversing the land sightseeing, hundreds of homes were washed away, and thousands of people were evacuated to safe grounds. It was a sobering realization.

11

CROSSING THE STREET

But that's the glory of foreign travel, as far as I am concerned…Suddenly you are five years old again. You can't read anything, you have only the most rudimentary sense of how things work, you can't even reliably cross a street without endangering your life. Your whole existence becomes a series of interesting guesses.
Bill Bryson, *Neither Here nor There: Travels in Europe*

According to an article in *Time*, the top ten most dangerous cities for pedestrians in the world are all in the United States. Yet, I never felt anxious crossing the street in Baltimore, Philadelphia, Chicago, or D.C., each in the top ten. Granted, I did get hit by a bicycle when I was crossing the street in New York City, which, surprisingly, didn't make the top ten. On the other side of the pond, I wasn't afraid to cross the street in Paris or Amsterdam. London gave me anxious moments when I forgot which way to look, but they have signs for thoughtless tourists to look right or left. However, the *Time* ratings of the most dangerous cities for pedestrians were based on the number of fatalities. What happens when the danger in crossing is posed by scooters, bicycles, and pedicabs? I may not die by bike or scooter, but crossing the streets in India and Vietnam consigned me to a state of panic.

Crossing the street in Ho Chi Minh City, formerly Saigon, was a dangerous sport. On our first morning in Vietnam, Susan and I were looking forward to our walking tour. Our guide, Thuyen, explained the rules. The trick was to walk slow and steady, not stopping in a panic or running in fear.

"Bicycles and scooters know how to gauge distance and will maneuver around you." I was supposed to trust that someone else was looking out for me.

"Avoid crossing in front of buses and trucks which don't have the same ability to slow down or steer around people."

Thuyen continued to educate us on Vietnamese driving etiquette. "Horns in Vietnam are not necessarily honked in anger, but to warn you that they are coming."

Standing at a corner in Vietnam offers a cacophony of horns honking, engines revving, and people chattering. I learned that all I needed to do to cross the street was to listen for horns, watch for trucks, move steadily, don't run, and pray I don't get hit.

After our lesson, Thuyen led us across the street for the first time.

"Follow me, and don't stop for anything. Just walk at the same pace as I do, and the motor bikes will miss you."

Thuyen was assisted by a "tourist security" officer who was standing at the busy intersection. The officer's job was to help clueless tourists cross the street. He smiled at us beneath his navy-blue cap adorned with an official seal touting his position. His forest green uniform with epaulets elevated his status from crossing guard to security officer, offering not only a hand in crossing the street, but also protection from disreputable taxi drivers and other con artists. But his most important responsibility was helping me get from one side of the road to the other.

Thuyen waited for a break in the traffic, especially trying to avoid large vehicles. While our tourist security officer started to walk us across the busy road like a mother duck crossing her ducklings, Thuyen guided us less confident travelers by taking our hands to get us started on our journey. Once we reached the appropriate pacing, he stepped back to assist the next reluctant traveler. I grabbed Susan's elbow and together we anxiously followed the others across Dong Khoi, the busiest shopping street in Ho Chi Minh City. I kept my eyes on the man dressed in green, trying to avoid looking at the motor bikes dashing toward us. It was an amazing dance, with scooters slowing down or speeding up to get behind or in front of us.

Lunch was on our own that afternoon. As we were leaving the hotel in search of good Vietnamese food, Susan and I bumped into one of our travel companions, Rubia, originally from Brazil, and invited her to join us. We had scoped out the Lemongrass Vietnamese Cuisine restaurant on TripAdvisor. Unfortunately, in order to get there, we had to cross a major road and this time we didn't have Thuyen nor a tourist security officer to guide us.

We stopped at the corner to plan the attack before crossing.

"Remember," Susan said, "we just walk. Don't walk too fast and don't stop in the street. We just go."

Rubia offered more caution: "Let's wait until there aren't any big trucks coming."

We paused, waiting for break in the traffic and summoning our courage.

"Okay, this is it."

In a leap of faith, the three of us looked ahead at our destination across the street and, without looking left or right, we steadily crossed to the other side. Our lunch of lemongrass chicken and shrimp fried rice was well worth negotiating the Vietnamese traffic.

Once we learned how to cross the street, although never without anxiety, Thuyen added more angst to the art of walking in Vietnam. Not only did we need to be cautious when crossing the street, but we also had to be wary of motorbikes and cars on the sidewalk. He explained that it wasn't unusual for a scooter to escape the chaos of the street by mounting the pavement. There aren't a lot of pedestrians in Ho Chi Minh City, and now I understood why. It's safer to hop on a scooter or a bicycle than to walk on the sidewalks where, not only might a motorbike join you, but you also had to maneuver around people getting manicures and haircuts, or even buying false teeth right on the pavement.

At least I knew which way to look in Vietnam. My fear of crossing the street also arose from the confusion over which direction to look. A lot of traffic around the world moves in the opposite direction of ours. Globetrotting around the British Commonwealth or former countries of the British Empire—England, Ireland, Australia, India, and South Africa – challenged my ability to cross the street safely. I greatly appreciate Canada switching to our side.

Ethnocentric American tourists will say that the Brits drive on the "wrong" side. There is nothing wrong with driving on the left. Ancient warriors rode on the left in order to keep their right arm ready for battle. It might be possible that the only reason the French drive on the right was that Napoleon was left-handed. As to why we Yankees drive on the right, it might have been a symbol of our liberation from England. Influence from France might also have encouraged our gradual move to the right. When Henry Ford placed the driver's seat on the right, it sealed the deal. I am not sure there is any truth to all this, but it sounds credible.

I appreciate that these "left-driving" countries have mitigated my anxiety by painting big bold white signs on the street. "Look to your right." Just in case you can't read, there is often a finger or arrow pointing in the correct direction.

It didn't really matter that people drive on the left in India because their streets are utter chaos with unusual obstacles to crossing the street. Like Vietnam, motorbikes were pervasive, but now I was also faced with rickshaws, ox-drawn carts, elephants, and cows, especially the cows. Our group of travelers was never given an opportunity to roam the streets of India on our own. Instead, we always followed our leader, Dil, who cautioned us about navigating unescorted. Dil took responsibility for crossing us, rendering a sense of security in the bedlam.

Our first day in India began with a tour of a Sikh temple – *Bangla Sahib* – where we also helped bake *chapatis*, an unleavened flatbread, for a community meal. Our city tour continued by bus, stopping at India Gates, a war memorial, and a former mosque. However, when it was time for dinner, the bus, although small, was too large to wind through the local streets, obliging us to walk the uneven passages in Connaught Place, a main shopping area, in order to get to our restaurant for dinner.

Often the sidewalk was only wide enough for one of us, so we staggered in single file behind Dil. She warned us of the possibility of open manholes in the middle of the pavement. Walking was made more dangerous by the heaps of the concrete lying on the sidewalk, signs of an unfinished work project. That is how we lost Marty and Mimi.

We made it to dinner without any mishaps, just a little tense walking and crossing. However, on the way back to the bus, as we crossed Road Number 6 from the Middle Circle, Marty lost his balance on the shattered sidewalk. Dil and Marty's wife, Mimi, helped him up, but as soon as he put weight on his foot, he howled in pain. Although Middle Circle wasn't accessible for tour buses, auto rickshaws roamed the busy shopping area, and Dil found one to take Marty and Mimi to the hospital. That was the last we saw of them. By the next morning they were on a plane returning home. They decided that walking on the streets of India was no longer an option.

And then there were the cows. Over five million cows roam the streets of the country. Sacred to Hindus, who make up about eighty percent of the country's population, the cows crap, eat, and sleep on the roads and pavement. It's not unusual for cars to have to swerve to avoid hitting one on the road. On our journey from Jaipur to Ranthambore, we stopped on a major thoroughfare to feed a small group of cows grazing along the side of the road. Dil explained that it is considered a sacred act to do so.

Our driver parked the van on the opposite side of the road from the bovines. As we attempted to cross the four-lane highway, we encountered countless modes of transportation, most of which had no trouble stopping to let us cross: a person riding a *Marwari,* a rare breed of horse with pointy ears that tip inward; a *jugad,* a jerry-rigged truck made from wooden planks and old car parts; and a camel cart. I heard Thuyen's voice in Vietnam encouraging me to keep a steady pace as we followed Dil to the other side of the road. Other familiar vehicles such as motorcycles, rickshaws, and cars also gave way to us as we claimed our path to the cows who were grazing near a water trough placed strategically close to the edge of the road in order to keep them out of the street.

On the other hand, I had no fear crossing the street at the most famous intersection in Tokyo — the pedestrian "Scramble" in the popular Ginza section of the city. Standing at the intersection, I waited in anticipation of the "Shibuya Scramble." All the traffic lights turned red at the same time, and everyone crossed every which way. I surveyed the intricate scramble before getting into it myself. I followed all the people in front of me, ignoring the others going in different directions. It was fun. Tourists go to Shibuya to partake in the ritual crossing.

As I was crossing the street I noticed an unusual sign on the opposite corner: Condomania. Above the sign was cut-out of a condom cartoon character, his head the tip of the sheath, with a large V-shaped smile. He was holding a heart-shaped balloon in his hand. I lost focus for a second.

But I couldn't stop with up to 2,500 people crossing all at the same time. Although there are five crosswalks, pedestrians are not confined to the painted stripes on the road. I made it safely to the other side with all the other locals and tourists and checked out the specialty condoms and novelties. I didn't buy any chocolate-flavored condoms, but I bought my two kids inappropriate souvenirs from one of the most famous crossings in the world. The store has since relocated a few blocks down the street. Perhaps too many people like me were distracted crossing Shibuya Center.

Being afraid to cross the street isn't irrational, not with scooters, bicycles, cars, and trucks coming right at you. Forgetting to look right instead of left is natural when you have been doing the opposite for sixty years. Undeniably, crossing the street is a cultural experience. It isn't wrong in other countries: it's just different. You need to "screw your courage to a sticking place and [you'll] not fail." (Lady Macbeth and later, Angelica Schuyler in *Hamilton*.

13

ILLNESS

"My psychiatrist diagnosed me a Hypochondriac. I said, "Okay, can you prescribe me a placebo?"
"Not for Type-2 Hypochondriacs," he said. "Your types would just fake faking. Then we'd have a real problem.'
Brian Spellman, *If the Mind Fits, Shrink It*

I am a hypochondriac, although the American Psychiatric Association no longer considers hypochondria a diagnosis. Rather, I suffer from "Illness Anxiety Disorder." I have endured this malady since kindergarten. In hindsight, my excessive absences in elementary school were a consequence of my indiscriminate anxiety. Nonetheless, the collywobbles were real tummy aches for a six-year-old girl. My mother enabled my anxiety by allowing me to stay home from school and showering me with attention when I claimed to be sick. On my fourth-grade report card, my teacher noted that I could excel in school if I didn't have so many absences. I hated Mrs. Hoey because she mistook my sensitivity and reticence for a lack of intelligence. I'd rather stay home with my mother.

At the age of eighteen, I almost missed my first international trip because of my imagined ill health. As the day of departure neared, my subconscious anxiety began to simmer. A sharp pain stabbed the right side of my lower abdomen. Concerned with possible appendicitis, my parents took me to the emergency room where a series of tests proved negative. The ER doctor didn't consider that I might be neurotic. Diagnosing me with dysmenorrhea or "lady cramps," he sent me home with instructions to take two Tylenol and perhaps try a warm compress on my belly.

My phantom abdominal pain persisted, intensifying my distress. What if I were away from home and became really sick? What if the doctor was wrong, and I really had appendicitis, and it burst, and I had to go to the hospital in Paris? I didn't want to die of peritonitis. My mother took me back to the doctor. I was half hoping that he might warn against my first globetrotting experience, but he affirmed that there was nothing wrong with me. I was going to Europe.

By the time I reached the airport gate the excitement of the trip started to outweigh the anxiety. I met my high school buddies, Karen and Felice, at the gate. Their enthusiasm was contagious. In a memory fashioned by a photo in my scrapbook, Karen and I joined hands, creating a seat for Felice, and lifted her in an adolescent display of exhilaration. We were teenagers on our way to Europe, and everything was a great, new adventure.

Not all of my travel maladies have been in my imagination, but my neurosis magnifies them. To celebrate my first birthday after my separation from Paul, I flew solo to London for four days of theater and sightseeing. I had a little cold, but the chilly, damp March air exacerbated my congestion, and by the second day I was miserable. Being sick is no fun when there is no one to take care of you – even more so across the pond. A hypochondriac like me can turn the common cold into a fatal disease. Could I die from a sinus affection? How was I going to fly home with my ears clogged? In spite of my lethal head cold, I saw four plays in the West End and took a stroll through the Tate Modern, crossing the Millennium Bridge, a pedestrian suspension bridge that connects the City of London with Bankside, about two years after its completion. My travel addiction is a formidable enemy of my hypochondria.

However, Athens did me in.

Ever since studying Greek theater in college, I had wanted to visit the Hellenic Republic. I imagined myself at the Theatre of Dionysus, standing in the middle of the proscenium with three doors of the *skene* behind me, each one potentially introducing another character from the great plays of Aristophanes, Sophocles, or Euripides. I would stroll into the *orkestra*, paying homage to Dionysus at the altar to the god of wine and fertility. I wanted to shout to the imagined audience, testing my formidable drama teacher's claim that the acoustics of Greek and Roman theaters rivaled modern technological enhancements.

I finally went to Greece four months after my cold-infested visit to London. Most of my friends at the time were remnants of my marriage and all of them had husbands, so I opted to take my second solo trip. I delved into travel brochures for Greece. Although the first internet travel site, travelweb.com, was launched in 1995, the old-fashioned catalogues were still the preferred means for choosing trips. I selected a tour that took me inland through the heart of Athens, Delphi, Nafpoli, and Olympia before boarding a cruise of the Greek islands.

Upon my arrival in Athens, I was met by a lovely thirty-something woman who reminded me of the flirtatious Lola in the movie, *Zorba the Greek*. She was holding up a sign with my name under the banner for Olympia Tours. Finding a person standing outside customs waiting for me always renders a sigh of relief. After the obligatory introductions, she invited me to her car for transport to the Athens hotel.

"Where are all the other people?"

"You are our only guest," she replied as though she were telling me nothing unusual.

"How can I be on a tour with no one else?" I was more concerned than my voice revealed. I was willing to travel solo, but my expectation was, unlike the long weekend in London, that forty other like-minded tourists share my journey through Greece.

"I am here to coordinate your trip. This afternoon you have time to rest and see the city on your own. Tomorrow morning you will be picked up by a motor coach for a city tour. You will join a group of people for a four-day bus tour of the mainland on Wednesday. After that, I will pick you up again and take you to the port in Piraeus to board your cruise where, of course, there will be lots of other passengers. Finally, when you disembark, you will find me waiting to drive you back to the same hotel for a relaxing evening before flying back home." A little relieved that I wasn't forsaken, I was satisfied with the plan.

When we finally arrived at the hotel in Athens, rather than rest, I explored the area, acclimating myself to the time difference. As I strolled the narrow streets of *La Plaka*, the oldest neighborhood that sits along the bottom of the Acropolis, I saw the Parthenon covered in scaffolding, a familiar sight from photographs. Continuing to wind through the store-lined alleyways, I found my way back to one of the two main pedestrian streets. By the time I devoured a traditional dinner of moussaka with wine and bread, jet lag caught up with me, and I headed back to the hotel for a good night's sleep.

Falling asleep was no problem, but when I woke up in the middle of the night to go to the bathroom, as I always do, I suddenly felt dizzy, so woozy that I had difficulty finding the toilet. At the risk of using a cliché, the whole room was spinning. Believing the best thing to do was to go back to sleep, I crept into bed, and, despite continuing light-headedness, I fell into a light slumber.

I had set my travel alarm clock with time to get ready and have breakfast before the city tour, but I woke up before the buzzer with a severe sense of spinning. As I slowly lifted my head, I began to gag and started retching before I reached the sink. I felt out of control. The vertigo wouldn't loosen its grip, and I continued to get sick.

Eventually, I managed to dress and walked down to the front desk. I can't fathom why I went downstairs rather than calling from the room. But I assume I didn't look well because when I asked the desk clerk to cancel my city tour, he didn't ask why. He did ask if I wanted him to call a doctor.

"We have a very good doctor who calls upon guests in the hotel."

I pardoned myself, reaching the ladies room in time to spew whatever was left inside of me.

"I would appreciate it if you would call the doctor," I said when I returned from the bathroom.

"Can I get you anything in the meantime?" he asked politely, in perfect English.

"I think I better just go upstairs and lie down. Maybe the room will stop spinning."

Neither the dizziness nor the vomiting abated before the swarthy, handsome Greek doctor knocked on my door. After a quick examination, he suggested that the air conditioner was making me sick and perhaps a walk outside might help. He prescribed a medication to stop the vomiting. I have no clue what medication I took, but it stopped the nausea immediately. However, the fresh air did nothing to alleviate the vertigo.

I rescheduled my bus tour of Athens for my return to the city in four days. However, I was determined not to let the whirling inside my head prevent me from exploring the city on my own, despite my woozy malady. This time wasn't as easy as it was in London where I could stand upright even if I couldn't breathe very well.

After a brief ride in the new metro under construction for the 2004 Olympics, I stood in Syntagma Square in front of the Parliament to witness the sentries guarding the Tomb of the Unknown Soldier. It was a bit of a disappointment because, with a slight drizzle, the honor guards were covered in a khaki coat rather than their glorious white *fustanella*, a kilt-like uniform with pleats that competes with any tutu. They still donned their scarlet fez with a black tassel hanging to the side. Capturing a photo of the guards while they rotated in my head was futile.

I tried to get a small bite to eat. Although the anti-nausea medicine worked, I didn't have much of an appetite. Finally, I gave in to the queasiness with a rest back at the hotel before trying to defeat it one more time with a visit to the National Archaeological Museum. My attempt to see the exhibits was a disaster. The English letters in the captions were out of focus. With anxiety mounting as I continued in the spin cycle, I started contemplating a return home. I walked back to the hotel confident that my trip was ruined.

I was down in the lobby early the next morning, luggage in hand. But I wasn't going home. Despite my foreboding the night before, I decided not to let a little vertigo interfere with my trip. I was the first person to board the motor coach which was making its way around the city picking up guests at local hotels. Still a bit fretful about not feeling well, I didn't take notice of any sites nor the people who were to be my travel buddies for the bus tour. Then, in what I can only describe as a miracle, the vertigo began to diminish. The further we traveled, the better I started to feel. It was obvious to me that I was allergic to Athens.

That diagnosis was never proven incorrect. During the four exciting days exploring the ruins of Delphi, the original track at Olympia, and the fishing town of Nafpoli, the vertigo never returned. However, as soon as we returned to Athens, I started to feel woozy again. It wasn't the air conditioner: it was Athens itself.

The next morning was my last chance to join the city tour. I was going — vertigo be damned. This time when the motor coach picked me up I was the last to board. I was thrilled to see people from our inland journey. Now, I had friends to take care of me.

The youngest guest on the motor coach tour was a 13-year-old girl named Zohar, from California. She was traveling with her Israeli grandparents as their gift for her Bat Mitzvah. As we disembarked from the bus to visit the Acropolis, Zohar noticed my unsteady gait and asked if I needed help. I gladly accepted the arm of the well-mannered teen. I was only 48 at the time. I felt very old. But, thanks to her, I made it up the Acropolis without becoming a victim of vertigo. I'm not sure if it was my unsteadiness or if I had simply seen too many ruins, but the Parthenon, entangled with silver piping, was an unqualified disappointment.

Neither my anxiety nor my vertigo lessened my excitement finally visiting the Theatre of Dionysus at the foot of the Acropolis. It was just as I had imagined it. I sat down on one of the steps of the *theatron*. Others joined me as our tour guide stood near the altar to demonstrate the astounding acoustics. I would have my own chance to vocalize later.

Many years before mindfulness became a popular trend, I sat silently and took it all in—the three-thousand-year-old stone steps, the proscenium in ruins, and the *skene* with its varied windows and door openings. I slowly breathed in air while suppressing the swirling still going on in my head.

The following morning, when my tour coordinator picked me up for the drive to the port for the cruise portion of the Greek adventure, I left behind a beautiful city in a fog of vertigo. By the time I boarded the ship, the sense of spinning abated, further proof my amateur diagnosis was spot on.

Seven years later I suffered *le malade imaginaire* on another solo trip, this time to the Scottish Highlands. I called the trip the "land of sheep and castles, castles and sheep, and a lot of green grass in between." I carefully documented my illness in my journal. After my arrival in Glasgow, sans luggage, I enjoyed high tea and wrote: "The food was quite salty and my health worrisome – more about that later." I fell prey to imagined ailments throughout my trip to Scotland.

On the second night I continued writing: "Last night was a nightmare. After sharing a bottle of wine with Mark and his mother (two guests on the tour) and a pleasant conversation with the two of them and Jan (Mark's wife), I went back to my room. I was exhausted from the long day as well as a bit jet lagged, so I assumed sleep would come quickly. It did, but a couple of hours later, I woke up with my heart beating fast and a pounding in my head that lasted for hours." A doctor probably would have diagnosed me with a panic attack, but I was convinced it was my heart.

I heard the sound of Poe's old man's heart under the floorboards coming from my chest. I considered dialing 999, the Scottish equivalent of 911. But, then I rationalized that my racing heartbeat was triggered by the large quantity of wine I consumed that evening. I prescribed myself a higher dosage of blood pressure medication and finally fell asleep as I crafted a note to my doctor in my head.

I sent an email to Dr. Ryan before sitting down for breakfast with a couple from Washington state who probably wished they had not had an extra place at their table. Part of being a hypochondriac is the requisite sharing of symptoms with others. I rationalized the need to tell another person about my condition just in case I woke up dead one morning. At least someone would know that I had not been feeling well and ask the hotel or tour director to check up on me. I regaled my breakfast companions, Craig and Linda, with details of my imaginary illness and anxiously waited for a reply from my doctor with his distanced diagnosis and treatment plan.

I checked my email every chance I had. There was no answer that day nor the next two. Our tour continued to Aberdeen where we lodged at the Ardoe House Hotel, the remarkably long-established Scottish home to Soapy Ogston, a wealthy merchant who manufactured, what else, but soap. The intricate interior woodwork was exquisite, and with the staff dressed in kilts, it was a tourist's fantasy. After a quick check-in, I paid a ridiculous fee to check the internet where I finally found a reply from my doctor.

Dr. Ryan wrote that there wasn't much he could do without seeing me. He advised if I were really feeling as poorly as I wrote (I wasn't), I should seek medical help in Scotland. I was disappointed. I thought Dr. Ryan had abandoned me, even though he was giving me the only advice that was medically sound. I swore if I died of a heart attack he would be sorry. I didn't die of a heart attack in Scotland.

When Susan and I were on our Peruvian adventure, we journeyed from Lima, at 500 feet above sea level, to Machu Picchu, at 8,000, and, finally, skyward to 12,500 feet at Lake Titicaca. The itinerary was built on the theory that if a person slowly ascends the mountainous terrain, her body will acclimate to the levels of low oxygen. Nevertheless, three days in Lima didn't do much to prepare us for the subsequent ascent, and by the time we arrived in the Sacred Valley to board the train up to Machu Picchu, I had a killer headache accentuated by pins and needles radiating from my skull.

There are limited treatments for altitude sickness: you can descend to a lower elevation, you can drink coca tea, and you can breathe in pure oxygen. However, as we continued to reach new heights, going back down was not an option. I drank the bitter green-tinted coca tea, although its efficacy to prevent altitude sickness has never been substantiated. I even brought home a few teabags as a souvenir. It wasn't until years later that I discovered that the still unused coca tea in my pantry is illegal in the U.S.

Altitude sickness pills only work if you take them before your ascent. Susan's doctor had prescribed Diamox for her, but Dr. Ryan believed the side effects of the drug – dizziness, increased urination, dry mouth, and blurred vision—weren't worth the benefits. My only option was oxygen.

Ronald, our tour director, carried an aluminum can that looked like spray paint. He sprayed the contents into his cuffed hands and instructed us to breathe into them, each time emptying more of the canned rejuvenation. It was oxygen in a can, and it was always available. As we ascended the Sacred Valley, we stopped at a roadside market with traditional Peruvian crafts: *chullos*, a colorful Andean hat with earflaps and a pompom on top, and blankets made from the wool of the alpaca. With an intense headache, I wasn't able to focus on shopping. Others in our group were milling around rather than souvenir shopping, complaining of similar symptoms. We required restorative oxygen. After breathing into Ronald's hands, I felt well enough to buy a pair of alpaca gloves.

Unfortunately, canned oxygen only offers short-term relief. The best treatment was a twice daily inhalation of pure oxygen that each hotel kept in its lobby to thwart the headaches and wooziness. With a lungful of air and a stomach full of coca tea, I set out each morning determined to revel in Peruvian customs and landscapes.

Although I continued to have mild anxiety about my health after Peru, I tried to mitigate my concern by forcing myself to be more logical. When a mosquito bite became infected, I still thought it might be MRSA, but I didn't run to the doctor. Instead, I talked myself into believing that the odds were in my favor. But then there was the time I didn't freak out about being sick during a long bout of what I thought was a severe case of reflux. In that case, a little more anxiety might have helped me.

By 2015 I had been a tour director for five years. Diagnosed with gastric reflux three years earlier, I had my heartburn under control with medication. I was on two back-to-back tours of the Eastern United States and Canada when I began to gag on my food and red wine. I didn't understand what was happening, but I assumed it was severe heartburn. Eventually, I began regurgitating whatever I ate. It was quite an unpleasant situation. Sitting in an Indian restaurant in Niagara Falls, I ordered one of my favorite dishes, chicken *tikka masala*, a mild dish with chicken in a creamy sauce, tinged orange with turmeric. As the waiter placed the food on the table, I gagged, not even able to take one bite.

Within minutes, I asked for the check.

"What's wrong? Do you not like it?

"I am just not feeling very well." The waiter graciously refused payment, and I quickly left after placing a couple of Canadian dollars on the table.

We departed Canada the following morning, taking the Rainbow Bridge back into the States and heading south to Pennsylvania. After a day in the land of the Pennsylvania Dutch, our tour took us through Washington, D.C. where I was able to fit in a visit to Dr. Ryan while my guests explored the Smithsonian Institute's museums. His diagnosis was the same as mine—worsening GERD. He increased my dosage of Prilosec.

Unfortunately, the discomfort and inability to hold down food continued, so on the next time through the District, I returned to Kaiser Permanente, only to discover that Dr. Ryan was on vacation. The unknown doctor who saw me suggested that I had a virus, and, that, this, too, shall pass. He gave me an antibiotic, just in case it was bacterial, and I returned to work on my tour. Nothing passed except the food that I ate. I wasn't able to sip wine without gagging. That was a calamity.

When I returned from my month on the road, I visited Urgent Care where I saw a third physician. Her diagnosis was asthma. What asthma possibly had to do with my inability to hold down food was a mystery, and, after the breathing treatment, I quickly threw up all of the medication. She didn't give up on her diagnosis, though. I was angry, frustrated about her absurd conclusion. I couldn't reason with her. After all, she was the doctor, and what do I know?

She prescribed medication and an inhaler and noted "asthma" in my health chart. I foolishly picked up the prescriptions. Eventually, I gave them to my niece who suffers terribly from what was my misdiagnosis. To this day, despite my attempts to tell a nurse or a doctor that I don't have asthma, it remains on my health chart.

I gave up trying to figure out why I couldn't hold down any food, assuming my anxiety was manifesting itself in a strange gastric line of attack. The symptoms eventually subsided. Two months later I was shopping at T.J. Maxx when I felt a sharp pain through my gut. I have learned that women often have different symptoms of a heart attack, including what feels like pain in the abdomen. Foolishly, I drove home and called urgent care who advised me to hang up the phone and call 911. This was it! This was the big one!

The paramedics arrived quickly to determine I was not having a heart attack, but they insisted that I be transported to the hospital where I was diagnosed with a failing gall bladder. Two ambulance rides and two hospitals later, my gangrenous gall bladder was removed through a four-inch incision down my abdomen. Three doctors. Three incorrect diagnoses. And a sincere apology from Dr. Ryan, whom I forgave. I wanted to report the third doctor for malpractice, but I let it go.

Then there was the time that I wasn't anxious when my friends and family thought I should be. I traveled to Cuba on March 10, 2020. I had made the final decision to travel just a couple of days before our departure. By then, Covid-19 had surged in China, Italy, and South Korea. The first case in the United States was confirmed in January, but we were told the risk was low. I wasn't overly concerned. Cuba had no cases, and the tour was departing as planned. 24 of us had originally registered for "The Best of Cuba: People, Life and Culture: Havana to Camaguey." Twelve people arrived in Miami for the trip. The following day the World Health Organization declared Covid-19 a pandemic.

We visited Cienfeugos, Camaguey, and Trinidad. On the fifth evening, as we were enjoying after-dinner Cuban mojitos, I saw our tour guides, Marissa and Elias, playing tag team on the phone. I knew something serious was going on, and the only thing it could be was that they were sending us home. The government declared the coronavirus pandemic to be a national emergency on March 13th, and it was decided to end the tour. We were booked on a charter flight back to Miami the morning of the 15th.

With only three cases of coronavirus in the country, each of them tourists from Italy, we wondered if we might not be safer in Cuba. However, the tour operator was concerned that domestic travel might be curtailed, trapping us somewhere other than home. By the time we left Havana after a quick drive around the city, one Cuban had been diagnosed with the virus.

I took all the suggested precautions on our return flight. I disinfected every surface I touched at the airport and inside the plane. I washed my hands often. I returned home just in time to be isolated like everyone else in the country. By March 30th, North Carolina issued its stay-at-home order, one of the last states to do so. Unsurprisingly, once I was home, the coronavirus stirred the hypochondriac in me. With every allergy attack or headache, I wondered: Could it be Covid-19? I wear a mask. I distance myself six feet. I order my food online. On occasion, anxiety can keep me safe.

13

TOILETS

[The bathroom is] "*the fundamental zone of interaction – on the most intimate level – between humans and architecture.*
Rem Koolhas, 2014 Venice Biennnale Exhibition

I am passionate about toilets. With a small bladder and nervous stomach, I often need to go at inconvenient times in out-of-the-way places, so it's important to be able to ask for a bathroom in any language. At 18, having already flunked high school French, I knew enough to ask, *"Oú est la toilette?"* I drew on my one year of college Spanish in several countries with success: *"Donde está el baño?"* The first Hebrew I learned in preparation for my trip to Israel was *"Eifo ha-sherutim?"* It didn't take long, however, to realize that a simple "toilet" in a raised tone clearly indicates that I am in need of a bathroom.

A trip to the toilet is a cultural experience. On our first rest stop on a long drive through the Vietnamese countryside, our guide, Thuyen, warned us: "Please do not expect to find toilets like you have at home or that we have in our tourist hotels and restaurants. Most of the public bathrooms in the countryside have squat toilets. Inside you will find a cup and a water spigot. When you finish, fill the cup with water and pour it into the bowl to flush."

I had squatted on earlier trips to China and Japan, but it's not easy without years of practice and it gets more difficult with age. However, most of those squat toilets I encountered on previous trips had a flushing mechanism. Here, we were expected to use a ladle to scoop water from a bin or a bucket to clean up after ourselves. It was the polite thing to do for the next person using the toilet.

People in many Asian countries prefer to clean themselves with a hand-held shower head that works like a bidet, considering water more hygienic than paper. For people like me who prefer paper, tissues or toilet paper are an essential item to pack before venturing out in the Asian countryside. I traveled to Vietnam prepared with a small roll of Charmin in my bag. I handed out numerous sheets to several of my fellow travelers. I knew from previous experience that the little basket inside what passed for a stall was not only for feminine products, but also for the disposal of the toilet paper. The lack of good water pressure and a poor drainage system can clog the toilet. Still, throwing the paper into the toilet is a difficult habit to break. I batted around 400.

About an hour after our rest stop, my small, overactive bladder decided it needed to be emptied of the bottled water I had been drinking. I carefully moseyed up to Thuyen in the front of the bus to explain that it was an emergency.

"Unfortunately, there really isn't any place to stop before our next stop."

"How long will it take until we get there?"

"Maybe an hour, maybe a little less."

"I'm so sorry, but I really can't wait." He had already warned us not to go in the fields because of possible land mines, so that was not an option.

"Okay. I understand. I'll ask the driver to find a place to stop."

On our original sojourn to the toilets, where we all squatted and shared a roll of toilet paper, the toilet was relatively clean. Now, even before opening the door to what barely passed for a bathroom, I was afraid I was going to retch. I was either going to pee in my pants or throw up, and I decided the second option was the better one.

The metal squat toilet was a step up from the floor. The tiled cubicle must have been clean at one time, but years of use turned the white plat-form into shades of brown. There was some kind of foul-smelling liquid already in the toilet, indicating that earlier patrons didn't do the polite thing. The red plastic basket had little paper in it. It was the nastiest toilet in all my years of going to the bathroom — a morose chamber of toilet horrors. Thankfully, I was able to relieve myself without losing my lunch.

Most travelers succumb to Montezuma's Revenge, or travel diarrhea, at least once on their adventures. The runs are usually caused by an unusual or contaminated food we ingest, but, in my case, it also derives from anxiety. My brain interprets the butterflies that I feel in my belly as pain, speeding up my digestive system to rid itself of distress. The collywobbles also release chemicals into my stomach, upsetting the delicate balance of my gut flora. The result is the skitters, Delhi belly, the trots, Cuban omelet, or the Aztec two-step. Several idioms for diarrhea take their name from the regions where dining out is considered risky business.

Raw seafood presents a particular danger to our digestive system. There is a good reason I don't eat ceviche besides that I don't like it. I don't want to invite Montezuma's Revenge. The night before we went to Machu Picchu almost everyone in our group dined on the dish of raw fish that originated in Peru. Ceviche is cured in lemon juice and seasoned with chili peppers and onions. Everyone agreed it was delicious, but I was glad to eat my well-cooked *lomo saltado*, stir-fried steak with onions, tomatoes, and French fries.

The next morning, we took the train from Ollantaytambo to Aguas Calientes and transferred to a bus for the final ascent to Machu Picchu. We stopped at the only hotel right outside the entrance, the Belmond Sanctuary Lodge. Our tour guide, Ronald, warned us that there were no bathrooms once we enter the ruins. Although there was a small snack bar and toilet right outside the site, the hotel offered numerous bathrooms without having to pay the one *sol*. Everyone made sure to visit the toilet.

We finally entered the lost city of the Incas with its steep cliffs and architectural ruins and followed Ronald along narrow ridges lined with grass escarpments until we heard a gentleman yelling from the back of our procession. Like the game of telephone, we passed along the message that one of our group members, Anita, wasn't feeling well, and her husband was on a rapid return to the toilet with her. She didn't make it, and I felt guilty that I took pleasure in the fact that it wasn't me. Anita never did see Machu Picchu.

Back at the cliffs, where the Amazon Basin intersects with the Andes Mountains, Ronald asked us to sit along the edge so he could do what tour guides do.

"It was Hiram Bingham III, a 35-year-old American explorer, who is given credit for finding Machu Picchu in 1911, although it was not a 'lost city.' At the time Bingham discovered the ruins, the area was already being farmed by locals."

I looked over to Susan, who sat with her head in her hands, looking pale and nauseated. When Susan looked up, I knew she was in trouble. Her face looked drawn in the sunlight, and she appeared tired. Eventually, she closed her eyes, and I could see that she was fading. Luckily, she remained in control until we were leaving the ancient site.

Susan's bout with the ceviche trots, a term I coined myself, complicated our considerably designed toilet routine. Susan, who suffers from significant stomach sensitivity, doesn't like to poop when anyone else is in the hotel room. So, after breakfast, she heads back to the room, and I, not quite as shy as she is to poop in public, use one of the hotel bathrooms. If she has to go any other time that I might be in the room, she politely asks if I wouldn't mind taking a walk. I read her clues well, so I am a frequent guest of the hotel lobby. On the other hand, she always lets me take the bed closest to the bathroom for my nightly visits. Susan is a great travel buddy.

Ask for a toilet in almost any city around the world and people understand. However, local idioms for the bathroom, like the toilets themselves, offer insight into the culture.

Although we speak a form of English in America, we have divergent terminology from Great Britain for countless words, like the "loo." The origin of the British colloquialism remains under debate. Many agree that it is related to Waterloo, although indirectly to Napoleon's defeat. It likely refers to the manufacturers of the iron cisterns that were used in outhouses in the early 20th century. Sitting on the commode, a lad or a lassie would see the name "Waterloo" engraved in iron. Perhaps the company's name was simply shortened to "loo."

It's also possible that the word derives from the French *guardez l'eau*, or "watch out for the water!" I couldn't imagine why anyone would watch out for water in the bathroom until I realized the phrase dated back before the invention of the toilet in the 18th century. Upon emptying the chamber pots from an upstairs window, the servant might call out *"Guardez l'eau!"* No one wants the odious contents falling on his head. A third, less likely theory, suggests that the term derived from Room 100, the common location of European bathrooms, eventually becoming "loo."

Another common term for the bathroom is the water closet. I have known of water closets, better known as the WC, since I read *The Diary of Anne Frank* in middle school. The WC was problematic for the residents of the Secret Annex since they couldn't make any noise during the day lest they reveal themselves to the workers below them. Some days a chamber pot would have to do. Other times they simply waited to flush. On my first visit to the Secret Annex, I was surprised by the artistry of the Royal Victorian delft toilet in its signature blue and white pattern. Two doves rest on a branch in the back of the bowl, crossing each other as though they are sitting on a loveseat. They are surrounded by a design of leaves and branches that continue on what many countries call a "seat." It's a small marvel in a heart-rending setting.

My favorite nickname for the bathroom on my travels was in Cambodia, although I think Adam, our tour guide, concocted it on his own. He called it the "Happy House." The toilets in Cambodia were the furthest things from a happy house, no matter how happy I was to find one.

Australia offers an unusual sobriquet for the bathroom. On our many visits to farms, ranches, and other remote sites, especially in the Outback, I found myself using what we refer to as an "outhouse," a small outdoor hut with a pit latrine, a "privy," or to Aussies, the "dunny." The term comes from the British "dunnekin," or dung-house. These are not structures made of cow manure, like those of the Maasai tribe in Tanzania, but, rather, a place to leave the refuse of our bodily functions.

I visited and photographed several dunnies, not only in Australia, but also in New Zealand. My favorite one was in the backyard of a local family we visited. The door of the dunny was decorated with a portrait of a woman, eyes closed and with the look of disgust on her face. Her nose was held closed by a blue clothespin in an attempt to temper the smell of the dung-house. Hanging from her portrait was a sign painted in a form of English: "A Place Off a Thousand Medition." Although the artist's English was a bit off, I got his drift.

New Zealand was a toilet-obsessed traveler's paradise. On our way to the western gold-rush town of Hokitika, we stopped at the Bushman

Centre, a quirky mixture of museum, shop, and eatery in Pukekura, owned by Pete the Bushman and his wife, Justine. Before we entered the building, Pete introduced himself and his eclectic establishment. We learned about his hunting skills and his passion for possums. Unfortunately, his possum pie and possum jerky were no longer served since he was cited for serving uncontrolled meat — he was killing and cleaning the possums himself.

The museum, which we could visit for $4 NZD, exhibited a variety of taxidermy and skeletons of critters, as well as traps and other hunting instruments, detailing how the Northern Island bushmen made a living. Finally, Pete encouraged us to visit the shop where we could pick up a copy of his autobiography. He also invited us to use the toilet.

The need for an invitation to use the toilet was revealed on its door: "STOP!" Under that were Chinese characters that I can only assume were translated below: "Our toilets are for customers only. Public toilets are 15 minutes North at Ross Township or 5 minutes South of Lake Ionthe. If you must use our toilets you will be charged .50 c. p.p. Please pay at the counter." That's about 30 American cents per person. Lake Ianthe, with an "a," not an "o," is one of the West Island's fresh water lakes surrounded by the lush bush. However, it was another sign to its left that made me laugh. "Please be patient even a toilet can only handle one arsehole at a time."

Unfortunately, Pete and Justine retired, shuttering the doors of the Bushman Centre, so don't put it on your bucket list. If in Pukekura, you will have to place your arsehole somewhere else.

Unfamiliar names for toilets are not limited to overseas. While waiting in line to enter General Washington's Mount Vernon home, the students encounter a small wooden building on the edge of the lower garden. Unlike most privies, its exterior strikingly matches the architectural style of the colonial mansion. If none of the students can guess its use, I give them a hint: it is a "necessary." There are always a few who quickly realize they are looking at the Washington's bathroom, albeit a reconstruction. Inside, which the students don't see, is a wooden bench shaped like a half hexagon. Rather than open pits, each of the three toilet seats on the three-sided bench is equipped with a wooden drawer that could be taken out to clean.

A young male responded: "Ewwwww...I wouldn't go to the bathroom with other people!"

"Haven't you ever used a urinal in a public bathroom?"

Another student, usually female, inevitably asks, "What if it's snowing hard or really cold outside?"

"Then the person could use a chamber pot that usually sat under the bed. However, the necessary was used primarily by the gentlemen. Women preferred the privacy of their chamber pot."

Eighth graders, especially boys, pay attention when you talk about toilets.

Unlike America, where using the toilet is usually free, I have traveled to several countries that require payment before peeing or pooping. I don't mind paying, especially since it is usually a pittance, but inevitably, I don't have the right coins or small bills. I paid to pee in a rundown corrugated metal port-a-potty in Cambodia. 500 riel. I was horrified until Adam reminded us it was about twelve cents. I took a picture of the potty.

I have used bathrooms where an attendant takes my money, allotting a few sheets of toilet paper in return. I had an encounter with an aggressive bathroom attendant in Thailand. I put a 10-*baht* coin on her tray, about 25 cents at the time. Either she didn't witness the payment or thought it was too much of a pittance. She followed me into the cubicle, pulling on my sleeve and pointing to the tray which contained a few coins and several *baht* banknotes. Since I had no more change, I gave her the smallest banknote I had — 50 *bhats*. I paid an equivalent of $1.90 to use the toilet and didn't even get any toilet paper.

Outside of our hotels and restaurants in India, we were expected to pay about the equivalent of 5 *rupees*, or three cents, for the privilege of using the toilets. I appreciated our guide, Dil, who handed the first person in line for the loo enough Indian *rupees* to cover the lot of us. A handful of attendants offered us toilet paper in exchange for Dil's payment. Often, they gave her a pile to share among us.

Independent travel offers the flexibility to use the toilet whenever nature calls. However, on a group tour, it is essential to have a bathroom break about every two hours and to use it when given the opportunity. Like Thuyen, one of my responsibilities as a tour director was to direct my guests to the rest rooms, preferably escorting them myself. On our first long drive from New York to Boston I gave the requisite toilet *spiel*:

"Good morning, ladies and gentlemen. I hope you enjoyed our New York City tour with Eddie. This afternoon we will be driving to Boston, about a four-hour drive for about 200 miles or 320 kilometers. I had to translate U.S. customary units into the metric system since my guests were premarily Brits, Aussies, and Kiwis. We will be stopping for a bathroom break in about two hours. There is a toilet in the back of the bus, but it is only for urgent situations. Rule number one is no number two. Please remember that whatever goes into the toilet stays there. Think of it as a bank deposit. It compounds over time."

Luckily, I usually don't need to explain how to use the toilet to my guests. However, on what is usually our first bathroom break on our New York city tour, I need to provide instructions on how to wash their hands. Until recent renovations, the bathrooms at Wagner Park, where you can also get a great view of the Statue of Liberty, had a button under the sink that had to be pushed in order to release a small amount of water to wash your hands. If you didn't know where it was, it was almost impossible to locate it.

Back home in North Carolina, my water closet, a separate room for the commode in my bathroom, is decorated with pictures of toilets from my travels, as well as some toilets on my bucket list. It is a testament to my toilet obsession. In addition to the toilets, dunnies, necessaries, and loos already described, my wall holds a lot of bathroom history. There is a photo of the ancient public toilets of Ephesus – 36 marble seats along three benches with waste channels below. Ernest Hemingway's home in Key West offers a more modern and private bathroom. The floor of his 1931-bathroom renovation is tiled with an art deco design in peach with alternating figures of ducks and fish atop a graphic pattern of white and black lines and circles.

When we were in Ketchikan, Alaska, I spent an unusually long time in the bathroom of Thelma "Dolly" Copeland, one of the first "sporting women" to make Creek Street her home and place of business. The brothel, established in 1919, was the only house served by a single madam. The toilet's round tank was unique. Without a sewer system, the waste was flushed into Ketchikan Creek, a spawning stream for salmon, and then out to the lake. However, the pièce de résistance of the bathroom was the bunting over the shower curtain. Having discovered that silk wasn't the best material for condoms, Dolly embroidered her shower curtain with flowers fashioned out of the silk sheaths. Although the city closed down the brothel in 1954, Dolly continued to live there until her death in 1975. I hope they had sewers by then.

When I returned to Heidelberg decades after I snubbed the bus driver in the bar, I had time to visit the university's old student jail, the *Studentenkrazer*. The 18th century building operated as a restrictive dormitory where students were only allowed to leave to go to class. The wooden walls and doors were covered with drawings and graffiti by the students who were guilty of such crimes as drunkenness, loitering, and the destruction of property. The cubicle was perhaps four feet wide, with four steps leading up to the hole in a wooden box, the "Royal Throne," as the students called it. A woman of a certain age, like me, wouldn't have the flexibility nor prowess to use their latrine.

There are a few pictures of American toilets, including one of my sister Reneé standing outside the door of a concrete commode at Eastern State Penitentiary; urinals in a graffiti-filled brick bathroom in New York, courtesy of my son; and the bathroom at the 21c Museum Hotel in downtown Durham, where I almost put on a show for anyone standing in the hallway.

My son, daughter-in-law, and I were bar hopping through downtown Durham on one of my pre-move visits to North Carolina. We enjoyed martinis in the hotel, which not only displays contemporary art in its restaurant, but also houses its own museum. It also has see-through loos. The glass cubicles with a toilet and a sink are completely transparent. The sign explains: "Privacy is just a click away. Lock door to make glass opaque." Having already downed a few martinis, I was perplexed. I entered the see-through cubicle and thought I locked the door; however, I could still see out. "Hmmm," I mused. "This can't be right. Maybe it's a one-way glass. I can see out, but no one can see in."

I began to unzip my pants and then thought better of it. Luckily, my daughter-in-law, Kristin, saved the day. She saw me struggling with indecision through the glass. She motioned me over.

"You need to lock the door to make it so you can't see through," she said.

In my drunken haze, I hadn't actually locked the door. I turned the knob and relieved myself. When I finished, I had to take a picture. The photo on the wall of my WC serves as a reminder of my foolishness.

One of my prized photographs is a simple toilet in a small cubicle with a few blue tiles down the center of the floor. Next to the toilet, which sits at an angle in the corner, is a red fire extinguisher sitting in a wooden box. Only a few people have sat on this commode, but when I took the picture it was Vice-President Joe Biden who did his business here in his congressional office in the Capitol. I assume Mike Pence enjoyed the throne for a few years. I can only hope that Kamala Harris puts a women's touch on the cubicle.

Finally, my most prized photo is of my dad. A few years before his passing, I drove him to visit his brother outside of Philadelphia. On the way home we stopped at one of the rest areas along the New Jersey Turnpike. By this time, my father was using a cane, and it was difficult for him to maneuver around the bathroom, so we went to the family restroom so I could help him get settled before giving him privacy. When we entered the bathroom, we both broke down in laughter. Next to the handicapped toilet was a miniature one for children. As my dad stood over the small-scale commode, I snapped a photo. Now, every time I look up from my throne, my father smiles down.

I'm looking forward to filling the remaining wall space in my WC.

13

FOOD

*I think food, culture, people, and landscape are all absolutely
inseparable.*

Anthony Bourdain, Interview with *CN Traveler*

"Food tourism is the act of traveling for a taste of place in order to get a
sense of place," according to the World Food Association. You don't eat
Kentucky Fried Chicken in Moscow or Pizza Hut in Beijing, although
I did both for reasons outside of my purview. I love to eat. I have been
accused of being a food snob: I don't do Red Lobster, Applebee's, or
Golden Corral, unless it's on one of my student itineraries, although I
must admit to having cravings for Chick-fil-A.

I discovered Chick-fil-A on a FAM tour of California. I had never
tasted their original chicken sandwich before traveling to Los Angeles
for tour directing school. As part of our two-week training, we practiced
our on-the-road skills with several excursions, including Hearst Castle,
Santa Monica Pier, and Santa Barbara. On one of our expeditions, we
were handed a lunch box with an original chicken sandwich, cross-cut
fries, and a bottled water. The lightly breaded chicken breast on a warm,
buttered roll was scrumptious.

My move to North Carolina brought me closer to Chick-fil-A with
a restaurant less than a mile from home. My ethos screams "boycott"
the place because of the CEO's public comments against the LGBTQ+
community and women's choice, but the chicken is truly addictive. I am
shamefaced to admit that my love of a fried chicken breast brined in pickle
juice eclipses my socially responsible behavior, and I don't even like pickles!

Before my son Joshua became a bigger foodie than I am, his food choices were limited. I worried about his eating when, as a toddler, he went through a period when he only wanted to eat hot dogs and chicken. His pediatrician told me not to be concerned: he'll outgrow it. He did. However, at 21, while his taste buds were still developing, Josh accompanied me to Russia for a camp staffing trip. Not finding the food in Moscow appealing, he opted for Kentucky Fried Chicken for lunch one day.

In retrospect, our lunch at an American fast-food restaurant in Moscow was still a chance to experience a sense of place. First, since neither of us spoke Russian and none of the servers knew English, we had to figure out how to order. We pointed to a picture and Josh held up two fingers indicating a two-piece chicken meal. It was auspicious that they gave Josh two dinners, instead, since the tiny drumsticks would have done little to satisfy his young male appetite. I'm almost embarrassed to say that after two and a half weeks eating the local food in China, I snuck out for KFC myself. I was the only tourist in the place, which was mostly occupied by local adolescents.

Pizza Hut in Beijing was a different story, especially since it was on our first night in China. Upon our arrival, David and I met up with our children. David's son, Eric, had already been in China for over a year, and our daughters had been there all summer. David gave Eric the choice of restaurant for our first dinner, and he chose Pizza Hut.

"Are you fucking kidding me?" I said under my breath, loud enough, I think, for Rachel to hear.

I added, "Why Pizza Hut?" in the sweetest voice I could muster, pleading to Eric to see the foolishness of his choice.

"It's one of the most expensive restaurants around here, and I can't afford to eat there on my own," Eric explained.

Rachel reminded me that I would be in China for three weeks, and by the end of our trip, I'd probably want something other than the local food: case in point, my dinner at KFC three weeks later. Eric was right. Our meal at Pizza Hut that first night was the most expensive we had throughout our Chinese adventure.

As a food snob, I not only avoid places like Red Lobster, but I also look down my nose at anyone who suggests dining at a chain restaurant, with few exceptions such as Bonefish Grill, but never when traveling. I want to weep when I see tourists standing in line at the Olive Garden in Times Square. Just walk up 46th Street between Eighth and Ninth Avenue, Restaurant Row, and you have your choice of excellent local fare.

Years ago, while I was still futilely searching for love online, I received a phone call from a gentleman with whom I had exchanged a few meaningless emails. After the necessary pleasantries, he suggested that we have dinner at Red Lobster and then go back to his place to have sex.

"You are going to have to do a lot better than Red Lobster," I countered to the bore who was no gentleman.

My love of eating and my addiction to travel first converged on my high school trip to Europe. Although the fondue craze had already taken hold in the States before we visited Switzerland in 1972, it was still in its infant stage. I had never dipped bread into melted cheese mixed with white wine and kirsch and seasoned with garlic and nutmeg. I thought our traditional dinner of Swiss fondue in Lucerne was bliss in a bowl. As my girlfriends flirted with the guys, I hovered around the *caquelon*, the earthenware pot that sat over a flame, keeping the cheese flowing like liquid gold.

Although fondue became the national dish of Switzerland in 1930, it wasn't introduced to Americans until the 1964 World's Fair. By the time I married in the 1970s, every bride received at least one fondue pot as a shower gift. I received three.

It's become trendy for tour operators and cruise lines to include home visits where guests can dine on home-cooked meals or enjoy native nibbles. I tasted *pavlova*, a meringue-based dessert topped with berries, for the first time in Australia and *gramoca*, a strong but delicious homemade walnut grappa, in Dubrovnik. I ate a golden kiwi for the first time in New Zealand, and I learned how to make *chapati*, an unleavened flatbread, in India.

Although some travelers are wary, I don't get the collywobbles about eating in someone else's home. Home-cooked meals on tour are a highlight of my travel experience. In fact, the feast we had in a tiny apartment in a Beijing *hutong* was unsurpassed by any restaurant.

With Rachel having already departed for home, David, Leslie, and I took a rickshaw tour of the *hutong*, an old neighborhood of narrow streets and alleyways formed by traditional courtyards, or *siheyuan*. David and Leslie rode with our guide, Nathan. Another guide, Duncan, drove me down the alleyways where generations of families occupied small apartments around a shared garden. We visited the home of Mrs. Ging, who supplemented her retirement by serving lunch to visitors like us.

The five of us sat around a table that barely fit in the small anteroom to the kitchen while Mrs. Ging served one savory dish after another. We started with Chinese cucumber salad, a simple dish of smashed cucumbers seasoned with garlic and mixed with vinegar and sesame oil. Spiced nuts sat on the table before the first main course of beef with potatoes was served. Our lunch continued with two additional entrees – chicken and peppers and a second chicken dish with asparagus. Just when I thought there couldn't be any more food, Mrs. Ging brought out delectable dumplings. Pizza Hut might have been the most expensive meal in China, but our home-cooked meal was unsurpassed.

I didn't eat the guinea pig, though. On our trip to Peru, Susan and I had the option of a home-hosted dinner, and, although Susan is a foodie like me, she wasn't interested in going on an optional excursion to a small guinea pig farm. Guinea pigs do not come from Guinea nor are they pigs. They are, however, considered a delicacy in Peru, where they are called *cuy*. Before signing up for dinner on the *cuy* farm, we were promised we wouldn't have to eat them – there were other choices. What we weren't told was that the cute, furry little animals would be scampering around our feet as the only two travelers brave enough to try the *cuy* dined on their meat, which, of course, they said "tasted like chicken." Nonetheless, if I were serving chicken to guests there wouldn't be any scurrying under the table. In a nod to our foreign taste, our hosts didn't serve the roasted *cuy* whole, as they usually do. Instead, they cut the small guinea pig into tiny pieces so that you imagined you might be eating a small Cornish hen or a very tiny chicken.

Although I like to eat more than I like to cook, I have prepared food all over the world. Soon after I started traveling with Susan, cooking classes became a part of our globetrotting tradition. Our first class was a cooking demonstration followed by lunch at the Culinary Institute of America at Greystone in St. Helena, California. Since we were learning how to make spring rolls and a couple of other Asian dishes, it wasn't an authentic local cultural experience. We just watched the chef cook, or, at least, I did. Susan fell asleep, which was a little embarrassing since we were sitting in the front row. But, nevertheless, we were hooked on cooking classes.

After our trip to California, we searched for hands-on, ethnic cooking classes on every tour we took. Our first participatory cooking class was in the deluge in Vietnam with Susan on the bicycle and me on the scooter. Despite the rain, we experienced shopping in the market where a vendor handling the leg of a pig eliminated any chance of my tasting pig's feet. After buying a wide variety of local fresh vegetables, we were ready to prep and cook.

Our first lesson was how to make flowers out of the vegetables we bought. Our meals in Vietnam had been filled with decorative food, and, although skeptical that I could create anything as lovely as the rose on my plate at the Lemongrass Restaurant in Ho Chi Minh City, I learned how to make an imperfect rose out of a tomato, create a flower with an orange, and turn scallions into leaves.

As we were about to start on the spring rolls, we were joined by a young couple from Paris. Now there were six of us – the Filipino couple from Canada who rode with us in the rain, the French youngsters, Susan, and me. We filled the wraps with vegetables we had bought at the open market, including carrots and cabbage, and added diced chicken and shrimp before frying the rolls in a wok. Our entrée was catfish, a type of fish that I had insisted I didn't like, despite the fact that I never tasted it. I think it was the whiskers. But after we added lemongrass and grilled the fish inside banana leaves, it was the best dish of the banquet. For our last course, we made *bánh xèo*, traditional Vietnamese crepes filled with shrimp and bean sprouts. As we sat down for our gourmet lunch, I not only had a sense of pride in my culinary skills, but I also enjoyed learning more about Vietnamese food from Dong and his assistants. Most importantly, it was fun.

The following year, Susan and I signed up to take a cooking class in Lima, Peru before meeting up with our tour. Sky Kitchen was a cooking school set up in the penthouse home of Chef Yurac and his partner, assistant, and translator, Christian. They planned a three-course meal for us to prepare with six other globetrotters from around the world.

We started with Peruvian tamales. It was Susan's job to press the garlic into the mix of pork while Jill, another American, added ancho chili powder. Susan gritted her teeth as she pressed down on the garlic, making for an awkward Facebook photo she quickly made me take down. I had the task of mixing the tamale filling. It wasn't easy, but somehow I smiled through the hard work. After placing a portion of the pork filling on banana leaves, Yurac demonstrated how to tie our tamale together with string. Each of us decorated our masterpiece in a unique fashion to ensure we ate our own creation.

The next course was the Peruvian culinary theme of our trip – *causa*, a delicate dish created by layering potatoes, avocado, and shrimp. The name of this traditional Peruvian comfort food derives from the Quechuan word *kausaq*, the indigenous word for "giving life." Using a four-inch-wide metal ring about two and a half inches high, we first placed the riced potatoes mixed with a yellow chili paste at the bottom, followed by the shrimp that we mixed with mayonnaise, and finished it with a layer of avocado slices. Like the tamales, we made our *causa* our own by topping it with slices of onions, parsley, and fresh chili in a distinctive pattern.

I was almost too full to eat our main course of *escabeche de pollo*, or chicken in chili-vinegar sauce with rice, but I never turn down food. We concluded our Peruvian cooking class with dessert: *trés leches*. I watched as fellow student Mitch, who was celebrating his last night in Peru with his girlfriend, Lizzie, poured the mixture of cream, evaporated milk, and condensed milk into the cake that we had baked earlier in the evening. We enjoyed our dessert with coca tea, just in case we were feeling a little light-headed.

The food tourism tradition continued on our trip to Sorrento. Susan discovered the Old Taverna Sorrentina Cooking Class online and signed us up for "Dishes of the Campania Region" with Chef William Gargiulo. After starting with Sorrento style bruschetta with garlic, tomato, and mozzarella, we next learned how to make potato gnocchi. With my first bite, I realized that I never had tasted fresh gnocchi. The slightly firm piece of dumpling seasoned with basil, tomato, and mozzarella, melted in my mouth. I swore that I would never eat frozen gnocchi again: it was so easy to make. I never kept my promise. Cooking while globetrotting is a lot more fun that cooking at home.

Our main dish was *chicken escapole*. Following the theme of the evening, Chef William helped us create a chicken cutlet that was topped with tomato, mozzarella cheese, basil, and white wine. For dessert we soaked ladyfingers in mixture of amaretto, coffee, and chocolate, layering two on the bottom and topping it with a mixture of mascarpone, egg whites and sugar. We repeated the process to produce a sumptuous Italian tiramisu. As we sat outside the Sorrento tavern at a tiny table perched on a cobblestone step, dinner became a sensual experience of aromas, tastes, sounds, and sights.

A couple of years after our epicurean adventure in Sorrento, I had a wholly different gastronomic experience in India. Susan doesn't like Indian food nor was she interested in traveling to the exotic country, so I traveled solo with a small group of other like-minded Americans. Without Susan to find cooking classes and given very limited leisure time, I depended on the culinary experiences provided by the tour operator, and I wasn't disappointed.

I had the most fun on a visit to the market place in a small village in Karnataka, in southwestern India. Our guide, Dil, divided up a shopping list for our meal that evening, assigning groups of two or three of us to purchase the ingredients with the 100 *rupees* she gave us, about $1.20. We had a brief lesson in Hindi: *Kitana?* How much? We learned to pronounce our ingredients like *tamaatar* (tomato) and *aaloo* (potato) before we explored the market in search of the vegetables.

Our odd group became an object of curiosity to the locals, both the vendors and the other shoppers. People wanted to help us. We were like pied pipers as we circled the small market, having no problem getting a good price on our vegetables with the help of our captivated audience. My purchasing partner, Barbara and I bought a kilo of tomatoes and potatoes – a little over two pounds — as well as carrots and some cilantro thrown in, all for under $1.20. Before we returned to our bus, our local volunteer shopping assistants, especially the younger crowd, wanted a souvenir photo for their efforts. Dil explained that we might have been the only white people they have seen. We were happy to oblige.

Our market spree was followed by a four-hour drive north to a campsite in the village of Abhaneri in the Northern India state of Rajasthan. After settling into our tents, we met Dil in the kitchen where she and the camp cook prepared our dinner, demonstrating the use of all the fresh vegetables we had each bought earlier in the day. Our market to kitchen experience, followed by local music and dancing, enhanced our stay in the rustic, yet splendid camp.

I also went food shopping in the local market in Taormina, Italy. Our group of seven ladies spent most of our first day in Sicily in a cooking class that started with a trip to the Central Market to pick up ingredients. The relatively small market included booths selling all of the foodstuffs we needed: fish, vegetables, dairy, and meats. We bought sardines that bore no resemblance to the ones in cans at home. These fish, common in the Mediterranean, were about twenty times the size.

We were invited behind the counter to choose our own seabass. As the middle-aged female shopkeeper weighed each fish, Claudia picked one up by the tail, posing for a photo. Eventually, Luca, our tour guide and cooking instructor, took a group picture, with Claudia and the fish in the middle.

The first item on the agenda for our five-hour cooking class was bread. After creating a simple dough, Luca encouraged us to be creative. "Mold your bread into anything you want!" Lisa announced that she was going to make a cat in homage to her kitty, Cosette. We put a turtle, a decorative bow, a pepperoni pizza, and a dinosaur, into the brick oven. The bread cooked quickly. After we each had a turn lifting the heavy pizza peel to remove the cooked bread, Luca announced he was serving it to his other restaurant patrons, too. We thought him senseless until we saw him breaking the bread into small, bite-sized pieces, obliterating all of our creativity.

I don't make a lot of homemade pasta, so, like the gnocchi in Sorrento, when we made *maccheroni*, I was surprised by how easy it was to prepare, and fun as well. Luca poured flour on the table in front of each of us. He instructed us to make a hole in the middle and slowly add water. After adding a pinch of salt, we kneaded the dough like clay until it no longer stuck to our fingers.

"Now, roll your dough into small pieces and stretch them out with the wire I gave you."

The dough looked very similar to the gnocchi rolls I had created in Sorrento. But, instead of cutting the elongated dough into small pieces to cook, we wrapped the thin dough around a wooden skewer. The next step was the most difficult, requiring numerous attempts before we got it right. Being careful not to close up the hole created by the skewer and not squishing the dough, we removed each piece of macaroni from the wire and placed it to dry before boiling.

Luca poured the vegetables we had cooked over our pasta and we feasted on *Maccheroni della Nonna "Sara"* or Grandmother Sara's Macaroni. But we weren't done. After eating our first course, Lisa and Liz worked with Giovanni, the executive chef, to create a masterful eggplant parmigiana with roasted eggplant. Nancy took charge of the sardines for *Sarde a Beccafico*, a traditional Sicilian dish of sardines stuffed with tomatoes, parmesan cheese, and bread crumbs and fried in extra virgin olive oil. These monster-sized sardines tasted nothing like their canned versions.

Next, the seven of us covered the seabass that posed with us for pictures with a mixture of salt and water that was baked until the crust of salt was hard enough to break off the fish. We sprinkled it with lemon juice and topped it with parsley and oregano. The bed of salt sealed in the natural moisture of the fish and enhanced its tender taste. We finished our meal with, what else, but cannoli, although we didn't have time to make it ourselves. It was simply delicious.

I call myself a "foodie," although the term is abused and even out of fashion. There aren't many people who don't like to eat, so aren't we all foodies? The definition of "foodie" in the *Urban Dictionary* mockingly clarifies its use: "A person who enjoys eating food, unlike everyone else, who hates food, thinks it's disgusting, and would never consider eating it."

I have, however, traveled with people who are more temperate in their eating habits than I am. There is an excellent adjective to describe these people, who include my ex-husband, Paul, and my dear friend, Carolyn: *abstemious*. According to the *Merriam-Webster Dictionary*, a person who is abstemious is "marked by restraint, especially in the eating of food and drinking of alcohol." There is no better descriptor for people who are the opposite of my indulgence of both.

Paul is abstemious. On our fateful trip to Savannah, we took a relatively quiet walk around the historic district. A little after noon I started feeling hungry, as typical folks do, and I suggested to Paul that we stop for lunch.

"We just ate four hours ago."

"Yes, so what is your point?"

"Is that all you think about – food?"

"When I am hungry."

After a quarter of a century living with Paul, I had learned to be assertive without being dismissive of him. I insisted that we find a place in an outdoor café and enjoy the ambience of Franklin Square as well as a bite to eat. We sat down at a small bistro table, and the hostess handed us two menus. Paul turned his over, as though to make a point.

I was in the mood for something to munch on – more bar food than a healthy meal. After Paul made it clear that he was not ordering, I ordered the nachos.

The waitress responded with a simple question: "Do you want the large or small?"

My memory might be fading with age, but I recall exactly what I was thinking to myself: "Even though he is not ordering anything, he is going to pick at my food. I will order a large one so that we can share, even though he says he is not hungry."

"A large, please."

"I can't believe you ordered a large." I was so taken aback by Paul's outburst that the exact nature of the next part of the exchange might be a little exaggerated or understated.

"You are a pig." I swear he said that. "How are you going to eat a large plate of nachos? What are you thinking?"

"I am thinking that you would share it."

"I told you I am not hungry."

"Yes, but that doesn't stop you from taking food off my plate."

"I can't believe you." And with that, he left the table and disappeared down the street.

I did not see him again until later that evening when we had reservations for fine local food at The Olde Pink House, an elegant 18th century mansion with Palladian windows, that has been serving traditional Southern cuisine since 1971. Paul ordered the pecan-crusted chicken breast, with classic local ingredients such as collards and a bourbon glaze in addition to the signature pecans. I, on the other hand, ordered the Habersham Platter: shrimp and grits, crab cake, and scallops. We never did talk about the nachos. There really wasn't anything else to say.

After a break from years of traveling with students, Carolyn and I took a trip to Eastern Europe. Like Paul, Carolyn eats to live, rather than lives to eat, although she still gets a sense of place from the local foods. It's the quantity of food we prefer that is different. It might be one of the reasons Carolyn weighs the same as when I first met her forty-five years ago, while I am three sizes larger.

I was always hungry when we were out and about on our travels; she rarely was. I spent lavishly on dining, but she preferred to spend her money elsewhere. While I ordered a grilled salmon steak in Prague, she sipped on a cappuccino. In the heat of the Venetian summer, we took refuge in a pizzeria where our friend, Špela, a former camp staff member, and I shared a mouthwatering pizza with artichoke, ham, and mushrooms while Carolyn sipped on her cola.

Toward the end of our journey, a former staff member from Hungary, Tamás, joined Špela, Carolyn, and me. We visited Predjama Castle, near the city of Postojna in Slovenia, Špela's native country. After a morning exploring the caves and the medieval castle built into a mountain, I was famished. We found a local restaurant with terrace dining and a remarkable view of the castle, *Gostilna Pozar*. The café served Slovenian food, specializing in crepes and other hearty dishes. It was a bit pricy. After all, it was a tourist restaurant at a tourist site.

After perusing the menu, Carolyn spoke up: "The next time I would really like to go to a restaurant that I chose."

I was flabbergasted, but her frustration had been building up every time my hunger led us to another expensive eating establishment. Carolyn walked away from the table. The three of us assumed she had taken refuge in the bathroom, but when she didn't return, I went looking for her, to no avail. Finally, I returned to the table to join Špela and Tamás and ordered *wiener schnitzel, dunajski zrezek* in Slovenia, where they prefer chicken to veal. It was served with boiled potatoes and sauerkraut, not much of the light lunch Carolyn preferred.

When I finally saw Carolyn walking toward us, I met her halfway.

"Faye, I don't eat like this. It's just too much."

She explained that she had not been prepared to spend the money we had been raking out for food. I understood. She had purchased what I perceived as an expensive painting as a remembrance of Prague. At the time I wouldn't think of spending that kind of money on art. Yet, my dining habits were extravagant. Some might argue that eating is ephemeral, but I consider it making memories, an essential experience when traveling. I promised to be more thoughtful about our dining choices. After all, she wasn't asking to eat at Pizza Hut or McDonald's.

My children, like me, grew into foodies, rendering them great travel buddies. They ensure the journey is full of good, local eating. When they took me to Nashville for my sixtieth birthday, Josh had researched the best barbecue and other local eateries. Our itinerary revolved around meals. We had a breakfast at the Loveless Café and lunch at I Dream of Weenie, a food truck serving the best hot dogs in Nashville. We went to the Barista Parlor for a coffee break and Peg Leg Porker for barbecue. We couldn't pass up one of Josh's favorites, so we had a lunch of fried chicken at Hattie B's. We ate Nashville at its best.

Before Rachel and I went to South Africa a few years later, she also investigated eating establishments in Cape Town, the only city where we had leisure time with options for dining on our own. On our first night we went to Harbour House, a seafood restaurant along the V&A Waterfront, the oldest working harbor in the Southern Hemisphere, that now offered a variety of dining, housing, offices, and entertainment. I ordered the kingklip, from an old Dutch word *koningklipvisch*, which means "king of the rock fishes," a savory delicate white fish that I enjoyed with some Sauvignon Blanc from South Africa. At Kloof Street House in the hip City Bowl area of Cape Town, a destination that attracts more of Rachel's generation than mine, I enjoyed a jazz brunch of roasted beetroot with a dukkah-spiced pistachio crusted goat cheese, herb salad, and a crunchy crostini, downed with a light cucumber martini. The live music and burning incense heightened the senses.

I lack one important characteristic of being a foodie: I am squeamish about trying new foods, especially ones that don't look like anything else that I have ever eaten. I am no Anthony Bourdain. I have foregone such delicacies as crickets in Cambodia and Mopani worms in Zimbabwe, although I tried the whitebait in New Zealand and the vegemite in Australia. I didn't like either one.

In his early memoir, *Kitchen Confidential*, Anthony Bourdain wrote about his willingness to eat anything, the weirder the better.

Do we really want to travel in hermetically sealed popemobiles through the rural provinces of France, Mexico and the Far East, eating only in Hard Rock Cafes and McDonalds? Or do we want to eat without fear, tearing into the local stew, the humble taqueria's mystery meat, the sincerely offered gift of a lightly grilled fish head? I know what I want. I want it all. I want to try everything once. (Bourdain 2000)

As much as I believe that food is essential to the travel experience, I lack Bourdain's courage. Come on, the man ate warthog anus in Namibia!

Rachel is my only travel partner who risks eating local food that others might deem bizarre. She ate the Mopani worm in Zimbabwe. She didn't like it very much, despite her protestations otherwise to the Bantu native offering the delicacy. She also tried biltong, a dried cured meat, in Botswana and sheep brains in the Marrakesh market, *Jemaa El Fna*, in Morocco. I stuck to the chicken, at least I assumed it was chicken. Unlike the worm, Rachel declared the biltong flavorsome and the sheep brains not bad. "They were quite buttery and well-seasoned, but a bit on the fatty side." Sorry, Bourdain, but I will pass.

14

A DIAGNOSIS

Nothing is permanent in this wicked world – not even our troubles.
Charlie Chaplin

My first night in Casablanca was the defining moment in my struggle with the collywobbles. Although I had previous panic attacks, my irrational fear of Rachel's demise on New Year's Eve in Morocco forced me to accept the fact that my anxiety was outside of the norm. I scheduled an appointment with Dr. Ryan, who was more than happy to write a referral for a psychiatrist.

My session with the shrink was less than comprehensive. He did, however, ask me a couple of questions before confirming Dr. Ryan's diagnosis.

"Does anyone else in your family have anxiety?"

After I shared that my parents and my sisters had been, at some time, on a series of drugs, including Prozac, Lexapro, Wellbutrin, Xanax, and Valium, he said it was a miracle I had gotten along as well as I had without medication. I was five times as likely to suffer from generalized anxiety because I have a close relative with the disorder.

The shrink quickly brought the discussion to its conclusion. "You have Generalized Anxiety Disorder. We can treat that with medication, but you will also need to see a talk therapist."

"What about you?" I asked.

"I don't do therapy." I wanted to ask what he did besides prescribing mind-altering drugs, but I stopped short, glad to have a solution that might alleviate my collywobbles.

He explained: "I'm going to prescribe Celexa for you. Although it's primarily for depression, it works well for anxiety, too. It's a SSRI or a Selective Serotonin Reuptake Inhibitor. There are relatively minor side effects."

I knew that serotonin was a natural substance in our brain that helps with sleep and weight loss. I didn't understand what was being "reuptaked" nor what was being inhibited. I thought that I needed more serotonin, not for it to be repressed. At the time I didn't really care how the drug worked: I just hoped that it did.

Within weeks of starting Celexa, I was experiencing less anxiety, but I was also experiencing hair loss, something I couldn't afford with my terribly thinning hair. Hair loss is a rare side effect, but I was lucky not to have most of the more recurrent ones: dry mouth, nausea, and increased sweating. Reducing the dosage succeeded in halting the hair loss while keeping the collywobbles restrained.

The doctor had also explained that there can be an additional side effect that frequently results from the medication – a loss of sexual desire. By 2011 I had given up on dating. I was willing to trade my sexual appetite for a sense of calmness in my life.

My first post-medicated international trip was the waterlogged tour of Cambodia and Vietnam with Susan. I joined the optional excursion to the Cu Chi Tunnels without her since Susan wasn't interested in a history, war, or tiny tunnels built by small men to capture and torture Americans. Our tour director, Thuyen, had already alerted us that what we call the "Vietnam War" is termed the "American War" here. Although his family was originally from North Vietnam, Thuyen tried hard to remain politically neutral. However, when he maintained that "Nobody invited the Americans into their struggle," two of my fellow travelers went into a dither.

On our way to Cu Chi, in an attempt to avoid any further unrest among us, Thuyen suggested that we might not want to watch the introductory video when we arrived at the tunnels.

"The video is an old propaganda film," he explained over the bus's microphone. "It tells the story of the tunnels from the perspective of the North and contains disturbing images." He said that, if we really wanted to view it, it was available on YouTube. I watched it back at the hotel. I was glad I did so in private, away from my travel friends who were having difficulty separating themselves from the painful history.

Upon our arrival at Cu Chi, we enjoyed a brief explanation of the tunnels before Thuyen demonstrated their diminutive size by disappearing halfway through an impossibly small hole in the ground. He stood there for a while, offering us additional history and an invitation to join him, although through a different entrance that was hollowed out for us Americans to fit. I would never have been able to squeeze through the rabbit hole that held him buried to his waist, not because I was claustrophobic, but because I was too large. In fact, that was the idea: the Americans outsized most Vietnamese people.

The descent into the Cu Chi tunnels required me to get on all fours and crawl through the dark space. I wouldn't have dared to descend underground in my more anxious days. The tunnels of Edinburgh were large enough to stand and walk around, and they gave me the collywobbles. These were barely wide enough for me to wriggle through. But my psyche had been chemically altered since earlier that year, and I was determined to make my way through the short passage.

As I burrowed through the tunnel, I was excited about my new-found freedom to explore, despite the ghastliness of the whole place. "I can't believe this! Look at me!" I had triumphed over my fear of enclosed spaces, although my new Vera Bradley backpack didn't fare as well, torn to shreds as it scraped along the tunnel's ridge.

In some cases, like the harrowing horseback ride up to the Maras Salt Mines in the Sacred Valley of Peru, circumstances proved stronger than the Selective Serotonin Reuptake Inhibitor. But earlier on that same trip, I conquered a fear of flying when we took a high wing light aircraft over the Peruvian coastal valley to see the Nazca Lines, giant geoglyphs etched into the ground. There were only five of us in the Cessna 206 – Carlos and Carmen, Susan and me, and our tour guiding pilot.

Carmen was anxious, but I was euphoric. As the plane ascended, I could look down into the valley without triggering the collywobbles. Carlos, who had traveled the world with Carmen, was able to humor her into a semblance of calm. It was Celexa that afforded me a new-found tranquility.

Our pilot guide pointed out the lines that took shape in the land-scape, including a hummingbird, a spider, and a giant. These geometric shapes were created by an ancient people by removing the earth and the rocks to form the design through negative space. At times I needed my imagination to see the design, like the monkey that looked more like a spirograph that I drew as a kid. Others, like the condor and the whale, were clear from above. Miraculously, these designs have weathered over 2000 years of history in the dry desert.

"These glyphs are believed to be the work of an ancient civilization that pre-dates the Incas, around 100 B.C.," the pilot explained. "The Nazca people worshipped the sun, the mountains, the earth, and the sea."

In order for us to get a full view of the geoglyphs the pilot circled around the larger designs. Although I didn't get the collywobbles, the whirling movement of the small plane caused some queasiness. Carmen was afraid she was going to throw up and grabbed a vomit bag from the pilot just in case.

As we flew around the hummingbird, over 300 feet long, we learned that it was a symbol of fertility and rebirth. I was confused. The only way that you can really see the glyph is from the air, and the airplane was invented thousands of years after the height of the Nazca civilization. I don't think you could figure out the design from the ground. Who could they have possibly thought would see their remarkable work?

Our guide interrupted my musings: "There are many theories about the geoglyphs. There are those who believe they were created by aliens, although that idea has been largely disproved. Most likely they were sym-bols created for the farming community, like prayers for a good harvest."

That reminded me of the Jewish celebration of Sukkot and its origins as a harvest festival. We hold the symbols of the holiday – the etrog (a type of citrus fruit), a frond from a palm tree, a myrtle bough, and a willow branch – and wave them together as a symbol of unity and faith in God. The giant man, the tree, the monkey, the flower – perhaps these were their ritual offerings to their gods.

Remarkably, I was able to look down at the dotted landscape, appreciating each design, even as the pilot made sharp turns to give us a better look. When we exited the plane upon landing, Carmen complained that she could barely walk. It was a rare experience in my travels to have anyone more anxious than me. I took great pride in the flying certificate awarded to me by the Nazca Lines operation.

Celexa helped me conquer my fear of heights two years later on the charming island of Capri. During a sojourn to the Amalfi Coast with Susan, we grabbed our overnight bags from our hotel in Sorrento and boarded a ferry to the Gulf of Napoli for a two-day outing. We stayed in a small guesthouse in Capri that was close to the beach and in walking distance to the *Port of Marina Grande*. While our room offered a magnificent view of the Gulf of Napoli, we had read that Mount Solaro, almost 2,000 feet above sea level, offered a must-see panoramic vista of the Amalfi Coast.

From the Piazza Vittoria in Anacapri we could either take a hiking trail, a climb neither Susan nor I were able to make, or purchase a ticket for the *Seggiovia Monte Solaro*, the chair lift. At first, confusing the chairlift with a funicular, I had no trepidation about the ride. I had been on many funiculars, from the one in Old Quebec to the Bica Funicular in Lisbon to the Hong Kong Peak Tram, but none of those enclosed cable cars with windows prepared me for the trip up Mount Solaro.

Seggiovia Monte Solaro wasn't a cable car or train going up a mountainside. It was a wooden chair, somewhat like a one-person ski lift. The chair was held up by steel rods that looked like a giant open paper clip while the timbered seat swung in the air, at times high above the lush underbrush and palm trees. Susan climbed on first while I mobilized my bravado to put my derriere in place and scale the mountain.

As soon as I was lifted off the ground I began to giggle, followed by laughter until, finally, I started to announce to the world that I was flying, and I wasn't afraid. I felt like I was breathing fresh air for the first time. I didn't know where to look first. I looked down at a strange vision of a black mannequin tending her garden, dressed in a sleeveless chiffon shift, her head covered with a white and red scarf. I wondered if a denizen of the mountainside was playing with us.

Even though the crossbar was not secured in place, I didn't wrap my knuckles around it in terror. Instead, I pulled it out and in, reveling in my freedom from acrophobia. I rocked my feet back and forth as though they, rather than a steel cable, were lifting me in the air. I was euphoric in my chemical serenity.

I looked in front of me, calling to Susan, "Turn around! Look at me! Look! I'm flying." I begged her to take a picture. I needed proof of my conquest.

As we reached the summit, we rose above the clouds to witness a crown around the mountain's peak. I looked in front of me to see the chairs disappearing into the mist, but my feet found their place on solid ground as we arrived at the summit. The locals call Mount Solaro *Acchiappanuvole* or "Cloud Catcher." As the air rises from the warmer base of the mountain, the colder air causes water to condense, turning vapors into a cloud. By the time we walked over to the wrought iron fence on the viewing platform, the clouds had dissipated, and the Gulf of Napoli appeared like Brigadoon, allowing me a close-up view of the landscape. My defeat of my fear of heights was complete.

Sometime after I began taking Celexa I stopped taking photos of the plane before take-off. I snapped a picture of our Korean Air Boeing 777 before Susan and I flew to Phnom Penh, Cambodia, later that year, but by the time we went to Peru the following fall, the pre-travel photo ritual to calm my collywobbles was superseded by pictures of clouds and mountains taken from the airplane window. They were a celebration of travel rather than an anxious attempt to secure a safe arrival.

Before my diagnosis, I developed a few coping methods for the anxiety caused by my new career as a tour director. I barely survived the first year on the road, but when I was able to invoke the perspective stress scale, I endured some of the more minor disasters. My boss gave me an infrequently granted second chance, agreeing with me that not all of the mishaps, from a motor coach accident to a brawl between two guests, were my fault.

Observing a stressed-out colleague on a different tour served as a lesson in how I shouldn't react. On our first morning in Montreal, my guests had dispersed to find a local eatery for breakfast and were returning for our city tour when we witnessed a German-speaking guide having words with the front desk clerk. Since I didn't speak her language, I wasn't sure what the fuss was about. When they switched to English I discovered that their group was served a continental buffet rather than a full breakfast since the chef didn't show up for work. Even though it wasn't my predicament, I thought the situation didn't deserve to be on the stress scale.

I observed the interaction between the tour director and desk clerk with great interest.

"You must serve my group breakfast," she shouted in broken English, the common language of everyone involved.

"We didn't expect to be without a chef this morning. We have done the best we can. You have yogurt, cheese, bread, and cereal." There wasn't much else the staff could say. I wanted to tell the German tour director to put a muzzle on it.

She continued to bellow about the breakfast, darting around the lobby, believing she was acting on her guests' behalf. Instead, she was raising their ire. I thought about my own behavior. There had been several incidents that provoked me enough to raise hell with someone, like the time decades ago when I screamed at the airline agent that she had to get my students on the next plane after we had to turn back halfway across the Atlantic Ocean. I must have sounded like this lunatic.

The proverbial lightbulb flickered. If the raging tour director would have insured her guests that they would have a lovely breakfast despite the fact that there were no eggs, potatoes, or sausages, everyone would have been a lot happier. I pledged to "look on the bright side of things." After all, as Monty Python sings:

Some things in life are bad.
They can really make you mad.
Other things just make you swear and curse.
When you're chewing on life's gristle, don't grumble, give a whistle,
And this'll help things turn out for the best.

Celexa helped me keep my pledge. Not long after I was diagnosed with generalized anxiety, I was taking a group of teenagers from our Newark hotel to Liberty State Park to catch the boat to Ellis Island. Although we left with plenty of time to make the drive, traffic on the New Jersey Turnpike was worse than the usual morning rush. We went nowhere fast.

"Is there an alternative route?" I asked the driver.

"Not at this time of the day."

I told him that I would call the boat to see if we can get a later time. He replied, "Thank you."

"For what?"

"Most tour directors would be screaming in my ear, yelling at me to get off the road and find a faster way. You are so calm."

I laughed. We got on the next boat. I knew I had succeeded at "looking on the bright side" when one of my passengers wrote on her evaluation, "No matter what happens, Faye always stays calm and fixes it." I finally got an "A." Still, now that I am retired, I am glad not be worried about taking care of everyone else.

Travel doesn't always have to be far. Months into the coronavirus pandemic, I booked a tiny cabin trailer in the woods of Asheboro, North Carolina for me and my pup, Zora. We could drive there without stopping, and we wouldn't be in close contact with people. She and I could sit around the campfire, take socially distanced hikes, and enjoy the forest view from the large picture window next to the bed. Friends questioned my safety, not related to the virus but about familiar past fears: getting killed by a stranger, meeting a disaster like a snake or coyote, getting robbed, and, an anxiety I have never had, being alone. The two nights in the woods were free from all fears except for a little rain.

The little pink pill diminished my collywobbles, but there isn't a pill to cure travel addiction. Even if there were, I would never take it.

AFTERWORD

*These so-called bleak times are necessary to go through in order to get
to a much, much better place.*
David Lynch, *Do You Have a Question for David?*

I finished writing this book during the Covid-19 pandemic. As I write
the afterword, travel is in limbo. On March 15th, 2020 our group of
Americans in Cuba was sent home to a changed world. At first, we are all
in isolation, quarantined in an attempt to stop Covid-19 from spreading.
Now, except for my one foray into the woods, my ventures are mostly
limited to the grocery store or a friend's backyard for a socially distanced
meal or glass of wine.

Leisure travel has ceased. The river boat cruise from Paris to Nor
mandy I was scheduled to take in April with my travel club was cancelled.
My trip to Argentina, Brazil, and Chile in the fall with Susan was, like
all international travel, put on ice. Most countries don't even want us.

I am not a religious person, but I toy with the idea that there is a force
that is screaming at us to slow down, to look at what we have done to
the earth and to each other. As of November 2020, over 250,000 people
in the United States have died from the coronavirus, over a million in
the world. These number change daily. In my naïve optimism, I believe
something good has to follow.

I also have to be confident that we will travel again. As the socially
distanced months continue, I have developed a new fear: *notripophobia*,
the fear of not having any travel trips booked. I desperately needed to look
forward to traveling. I considered the safest destinations, ones where the
virus has been controlled: New Zealand, Turkmenistan, and Switzerland,
among others. Europe seems to be a crap shoot, so I chose a tour to some

of the most out-of-the-way destinations – Bhutan, Nepal, and Tibet. I am waiting for a vaccine. A trip can always be cancelled.

I am afraid to wait too long to travel again. I am worried that my rapidly aging body will be a stronger deterrent than the collywobbles. Some of my friends, including Susan, say their travel days are over. I have been able to control my anxiety, but it is not as easy to fight arthritis. I am determined to hike the two miles up the precarious dirt trail along the mountainside to the Tiger's Nest Monastery, *Paro Takstang*, a small collection of temples perched 10,320 feet high. I can take some Advil and Lyrica to give my body a push, and Diomax for the altitude sickness, but, like conquering anxiety, I need additional skills. I have one year and two walking sticks to gain the strength and agility to climb. Next year in Bhutan.

ACKNOWLEDGEMENTS

Collywobbles was, in many ways, a cooperative effort, and I am greatly appreciative of all my family, travel buddies, friends, tour guide colleagues, and Facebook friends for their patience and input.

Thank you to my family. My children, Joshua Bousel and Rachel Bousel, and their spouses, Kristin Resurreccion and Chuck Flores, all of whom share my love of travel. To my former husband and now friend, Paul Bousel, for encouraging me to tell my story and being a good sport about it. I am glad that he has found happiness with his soulmate, Merrilee Seidman. In loving memory of my parents, Melvin and Cecile Brenner, who gave birth to my wanderlust by sending me to Europe in high school.

I have had numerous travel buddies throughout my globetrotting, each of whom made me a better traveler. Thank you to my teachers, Victor Jaccarino and Arthur Siegel (of blessed memory), who not only showed me the world, but also let us teenage girls experience it on our own. I started traveling the world with Carolyn Kreiter Foronda at age 26 and continued for over thirty years. She taught me to how to look at art and read poetry. My best buddy, Susan Cohen, taught me how to have fun and let go of my anxiety as we traveled the United States, Canada, Central America, Asia, and Europe. I have known Janet Muenz since our children were infants, but we only started traveling together later in life. Janet and I share a remarkable similarity of taste, making her a fabulous travel buddy.

Thank you to all my other travel partners who not only shared my wanderlust, but also helped fill in the details for this book. My sisters – Jeanne Schnell and Renee Devantier; my good friends – Wendy Weisbard and Terry Cuzzolino; my camp friends—Betty Balin, Fran Leibowitz,

Jill Epstein, Špela Repic, Támas Uhrin, Agnieszka Beger, and Martin Vrabec; my school friends – Linda Cable, Wendy Vu, and Randi Adleberg; my tour director friends—Deby Dahlgren and Scott Dworkin; my community friends—Scarlett and Larry Wilson, Lisa Scacco, and Nancy Scacco. I offer apologies to the many unnamed others who answered Facebook posts, desperate emails, and numerous texts.

I want to acknowledge the professional tour directors who showed me the world. Each one enhanced my travel experience. A few stand-outs include Tim from England; Chris, also from England; Norman from Austria; Colleen from England, but who took us all through Scandinavia; Gillian Perry, also from England; Dorina from Greece; Manuel from Portugal; Dil from India; Ronald from Peru, Dianne from New Zealand, Rolando from Costa Rica; Hassan from Morocco; Ezra from Israel; Nathan from China; Marissa from Florida, but who took us around Cuba with our Cuban guide, Elias; Richard from Scotland; Adam from Cambodia; Thuyen from Vietnam; Colin from Belgium; Rosario from Sicily; Mr. Mony at Angor Wat; and Reiko Konishi from Japan.

Thank you to all my friends who willingly or begrudgingly read the book over the years and helped me develop my stories and make sure this English teacher's grammar and spelling were acceptable: Debra Hoffman, Deb Kantrowitz, Randy Warren, Carolyn Kreiter Foronda, Susan Cohen, Lisa Scacco, Eileen Waskowicz, and Barbara Elish, who edited my website: www.fayebrenner.com.

Dr. Christopher Ryan, my family doctor for almost twenty years, deserves my gratitude for always listening; for his empathy, especially on the passing of my mother and through my father's many illnesses; and, most of all, for his insistence that I suffered from anxiety. He changed the way I travel and live. I also want to thank my current therapist who, although she prefers anonymity, has helped me find my voice.

Last, but certainly not least, a big shout out to my editor, Sally Stotter, who also shares my wanderlust. Thank you to Debra Hoffman, again, for copy editing the last draft. Finally, I want to show my greatest appreciation to my friend of over fifty years, Karen Strauss, who lent me her professional expertise and guided me through the publication of this book.

CPSIA information can be obtained
at www.ICGtesting.com
Printed in the USA
LVHW081336130121
675965LV00008B/168